"In *The 3 Minute Window: 52 Ways to Inject the Gospel into Every Message*, EvanTell's founder and CEO, Larry Moyer, not only offers pastors fifty-two prompts to infuse the gospel into the sermons they preach, but he helps them to craft gospel invitations that flow out of the texts they preach. His brief, three minute gospel presentations from selected Old and New Testament texts provide pastors with a line of sight through the gospel window of their texts, in order that their hearers might be invited to enter through the open door of the gospel."

— MATT QUEEN

Associate Professor and L. R. Scarborough Chair of Evangelism ("The Chair of Fire") Associate Dean of the Roy J. Fish School of Evangelism and Missions Southwestern Baptist Theological Seminary, Fort Worth, Texas

---

"Whenever I come across a worthwhile discussion of a scripture passage in my reading, I file the author, book, and page number of that discussion in a computer folder I've created for biblical references. If I ever preach on that passage years later, I refer to that folder to see what entries I have on that passage. Guess what I'm going to do with the passages Larry has at the start of each of his chapters? Yep—I'm going to file them, so that later I'll have some expert guidance on how to weave the gospel into my message on that passage."

— DONALD R. SUNUKJIAN

Professor of Preaching, Talbot School of Theology

GH00499776

THE 3 MINUTE WINDOW

52 ways to inject the gospel into every message

R. LARRY MOYER

*Dedicated to church leaders across the world
who want to reach out to unbelievers every
Sunday with a gospel presentation that is clear,
positive, relevant, and different.*

Contents

Introduction   i

1. As a Parent, Tell Your Child About Someone You Know, Not Someone You Know About   1

2. Bad News, Good News   3

3. Christianity is about a Message, Not a Messenger   5

4. "Come" Tells Us How Many People God Cares For   7

5. Come to Christ and You Will Get Two for the Price of One   9

6. Come to God and You Will Meet the Promise-Keeper, Not the Promise-Breaker   11

7. Do vs. Done   13

8. Do Yourself a Favor   15

9. Don't Put Off until Tomorrow What You Should Do Today   17

10. Don't Worry about Parts of the Bible You Don't Understand; Worry about Those You Do   19

11. Every Marriage Needs a Third Person–of the Right Kind   21

12. God Actually is Unfair   23

13. God Has a Reputation for Making Miracles
    out of Messes   25

14. God's Greatest Desire for Your Life   27

15. God's Love is Not "Iffy"   29

16. Hope So or Know So Salvation   31

17. It's Your Move   33

18. Mislabeling Can Be Dangerous   35

19. Nothing Is Worth Being Separated from
    God Over   37

20. One Gift You Can Never Lose   39

21. One Question the Bible Answers Clearly   41

22. Only Jesus Christ Can Break Your Chains   43

23. Salvation is Not Christ Plus, but Christ Period   45

24. Satan's Primary Goal in Your Life   47

25. Satisfaction is Found in a Person, not
    Possessions   49

26. Talk to the Person Who Lives There   51

27. The Best Definition and Example of Love   53

28. The Best is Yet to Come   55

29. The Best Way I Can Use My Tongue   57

30. The Biggest Difference Between Religion
and Christ   59

31. The Day You Die Ought to be More Exciting
than the Day You Were Born   61

32. The Greatest Formula in the Bible   63

33. The Lord's Table Looks Three Ways   65

34. The Mark of a True Friend   67

35. The Most Humble Person You Will Ever Meet   69

36. The Most Important Word in the Christmas Story   71

37. The One Thing that Stands Between You and God   73

38. The Past Can Be a Memory, Not a Nightmare   75

39. The People You are Attracted to the Most   77

40. The Truth Hurts, But It Also Helps   79

41. Three Questions God is Not Asking You   81

42. Three Things God Cannot Do   83

43. Two Kinds of Religion   85

44. Wealth is Not What You Have But Who You Know   87

45. "Who Am I" Can Be Answered in Six Words   89

46. With God, there is No Longer a Need for "If Only"   91

47. You Are Never Too Big a Sinner for God to Save   93

48. You Can Overcome the Fear of Dying   95

49. You Cannot Live the Christian Life   97

50. Your Final Address   99

51. Your Goodness is Not Good Enough   101

52. Your Struggle is from God   103

Introduction

The job of the church is to build up believers to do the work of the ministry. As Ephesians 4:12-13 explains, we are here *"for the equipping of the saints for the work of the ministry, for the edifying of the body of Christ, till we all come to the unity of the faith and of the knowledge of the Son of God, to a perfect man, to the measure of the stature of the fullness of Christ."*

For this reason, not every message a pastor gives can be directed towards non-Christians. If it were, the church would be full of people who are shallow spiritually—who have learned how to *enter* the Christian life but know very little about how to *live* it. At the same time, every pastor needs to be aware that on any given Sunday, there are those in attendance who may have never met the Savior. So how does one reach out to unbelievers without losing the thrust of a well-developed message aimed at believers?

One way is to do so at the end of your message, perhaps even during the closing prayer. It is effective to say, "Now my message has been directed to those who know the Lord. But maybe you are here, and you do not know for certain that, if you were to die, you would go to heaven. The Bible makes the plan of salvation very clear and simple." Then give a brief but clear explanation of the gospel and invite them to respond.

Another way is to inject the truth of salvation wherever in the course of a message it would be appropriate to do so. One may be speaking about love, sacrifice, the results of sin, death, substitution, humility, victory, marriage, parenting, eternal life, or a host of other subjects. Topics such as those provide an opportunity to give a brief explanation of the gospel.

When doing this every Sunday, it must be done with variety—otherwise it will cease to draw attention and lose its meaning. Years ago, I was challenged as an evangelist who enjoys equipping church leaders to come up with 52 different presentations of the gospel: ones that would be appropriate for any Sunday, a communion Sunday, particular holidays, etc. Ones that would be appropriate whether they are watching the service online, or actually seated in the congregation. In other words, 52 different ways of telling people what we must understand to come to Christ: that we are sinners, Christ died for our sins and rose again, and we have to trust Christ – sin, substitution, and faith. It is my hope that these presentations will help you in your outreach to unbelievers. An added benefit will be that you will show your people how to share the gospel in different ways and even be modeling the need to do so. You will thus lead your people in evangelism through example, not merely exhortation.

I use selected passages of Scripture with each presentation. Keep in mind though that there are a variety of other passages you could choose to use to convey the same ideas. I hope this book serves to show you that regardless of the text from which you are speaking, there is always a very effective and smooth way you can inject a clear presentation of the gospel.

Please understand that you can close these presentations any way you like as you invite them to come to the Savior, whether that is by seeing you after the service, raising their hand to indicate they would like to talk to you, noting on a card that they wish to become a Christian, or coming forward during a service.

I have left it up to you as to how you wish to identify those who are interested. These are simply 52 different ways to explain the message of the gospel—that Christ died for your sins and rose from the dead.

It's important to realize that although stated here in book-form, these 52 presentations have been written in the style of the *speaking-voice* since they are to be delivered from the pulpit. Each one has been constructed with a three-minute "window" in mind.

Do unbelievers a favor. Even if your message is not directed to them, reach out to them during your message or at the end of the service in a way that is warm, clear, and inviting. Through such a brief moment, God could do something eternal - He could bring them to the Savior, or at least one step closer to the cross.

1

As a Parent, Tell Your Child About Someone You Know, Not Someone You Know About

(using Ephesians 6:4)

Raising children is one of life's toughest assignments. God helps us by telling us how it ought to be done.

In Ephesians 6:4, God says, "And you, fathers, do not provoke your children to wrath, but bring them up in the training and admonition of the Lord." Although speaking specifically to fathers, both fathers and mothers play a part in child-rearing.

In a positive and encouraging way, we are to raise our children in a way that they understand His teaching, and how they can live a life that honors God.

That brings every parent to something very sobering and thought-provoking. If you are going to teach a child how to live for God, you yourself have to know God, not just know *about* God. It is difficult to introduce your child to someone who you don't personally know.

But knowing God does not mean going to a church where people worship Him, spending a few moments in prayer each day, or reading a portion of His Word on a frequent basis. Knowing God is something very deep and personal. It is being certain that you have a relationship with God and will live with Him forever. He is not just the Savior; He is *your* Savior.

That requires an understanding that as your children will rebel against you, you have likewise rebelled against God.

In thoughts, words, or actions, you have been disobedient. As you must punish your children when they do wrong, God has to punish sin. That punishment is death and eternal separation from God. But God loves you far more than you even love your children. He sent His Son into the world to die in your place as your substitute and to rise again the third day.

Because His Son died for you, God can now pardon you instead of punishing you. You receive that pardon by simple faith, trusting Christ alone to get you to heaven. The moment you trust Christ you are personally related to God. You don't just know about God, you *know* Him.

As you prepare to teach your children how to honor God, begin by asking yourself the question, "Do I know about God, or do I know God?" Have you trusted Christ to save you?

2

Bad News, Good News

(Using Romans 3:23, 6:23. 5:8, Ephesians 2:8,9)

The greatest need in the world is to know that when you die you are going to be in God's presence forever. But to understand how you can know that, you must know there is some bad news and some good news. The bad news is something about you. The good news is something about God.

The bad news is that you and I are sinners. Romans 3:23 of the Bible tells us, "For all have sinned and fall short of the glory of God." God's standard is perfection. But every one of us has sinned and can't measure up to that standard. In thoughts, words, and deeds, we have not been perfect and never will be.

That bad news gets worse. Three chapters later in Romans 6:23, the Bible says, "For the wages of sin is death." Because we have sinned, we deserve to die and be forever separated from God.

But there is good news! Since there was no way we could come to God, the Bible says that God decided to come to us. The good news is that Jesus Christ, God's perfect Son came into the world, took your sin and my sin, your punishment and my punishment, placed it upon Himself and died for us. The Bible tells us in Romans 5:8, "But God demonstrates His own love toward us, in that while we were still sinners, Christ died for us." The third day He rose again, proving His victory over sin and the grave.

3

Just as the bad news kept getting worse, the good news keeps getting better. Because the price for our sin has been paid, we can now be saved through faith. In Ephesians 2:8-9 we are told, "For by grace you have been saved through faith, and that not of yourselves; it is the gift of God, not of works, lest anyone should boast." That word faith means *trust*. Just as you sit down in a chair and trust the chair to hold you, you must place your trust in Christ alone as your only way to heaven. The moment you do, God gives you eternal life as a completely free gift.

So, if you understand the bad news and the good news, you ought to ask yourself the question, "What's keeping me from trusting Christ right now?" Don't put off until tomorrow, what should be done today.

3

Christianity is about a Message, Not a Messenger

(using 1 Corinthians 15:3-5, Isaiah 53:5, Psalms 16:10)

Many who contemplate becoming Christians are turned off by those who claim to know Him. Their lives and actions don't seem appropriate for those who label themselves as "Christians."

Careful. As unfortunate as that is, you must understand that Christianity is about a message, not the messengers. The most perfect Christian cannot change your eternal destiny; the message can.

That message is contained in 1 Corinthians 15:3-5. "For I delivered to you first of all that which I also received: that Christ died for our sins according to the Scriptures, and that He was buried, and that He rose again the third day according to the Scriptures, and that He was seen by Cephas, then by the twelve."

That one sentence tells us four things about Christ.

One: *Christ died for our sins.* "For" means "on behalf of." Christ took our place on a cross, suffering the punishment that we deserved. He substituted His life for ours. Isaiah 53:5 predicted His death when it says, "He was wounded for our transgressions, He was bruised for our iniquities."

Secondly, we are told *He was buried* – that is the proof that He died.

The third fact about Christ is *He rose again the third day.* Psalm 16:10 predicted His resurrection when it says, "For You will not leave my soul in Sheol, Nor will You allow Your Holy One to see corruption." His resurrection proved that God had accepted what His Son did as sufficient payment for our sins.

Finally, we are told *He was seen*. The greatest evidence you can have in court is an eyewitness. Just as His burial proved that He died, the fact that He was seen proved He arose.

Those four facts could be reduced to ten words commonly called the Good News – *Christ died for our sins and rose from the dead*. That is the message – the most exciting news you will ever hear. Because if you will come to God in simple faith, trusting Him alone as your only way to heaven, God will give you completely free His gift of eternal life.

It is all about a message, not a messenger. Don't get so distracted by a messenger that you miss the message that has changed millions of lives and can change yours – Christ died for your sins and rose from the dead.

4

"Come" Tells Us How Many People God Cares For

(Using Matthew 11:28, 2 Corinthians 5:15)

Jesus once said, "Come to Me, all you who labor and are heavy laden, and I will give you rest." By that He meant if you come to Him, you will find the most peaceful life known to man. For the first time ever, you will know you are going to heaven. And as you learn more about Him, He will show you how to live a life of fulfillment instead of frustration.

The greatest word in that entire invitation Christ gave has to be the word "come." That word has no exception clause after it. The reason is nobody is excluded. God wants *all* to come to Him – every child, every teenager, everyone of middle age, all who are elderly—*everyone*. It may be a child who is nine or an adult who is ninety. Personal circumstances, background, criminal record, reputation, or how others feel about you – none of that matters. The reason is there are nobody's sins for whom He did not die.

2 Corinthians 5:15 contains an interesting phrase. The first five words of that verse are "and He died for all." There is no one who is not a sinner, and there is no one who does not deserve to pay for his sin through eternal separation from God. There is no one who can earn his way to heaven by being good or doing right. That is why, in order to receive everyone who desires eternal life, when Jesus Christ died on the cross, He had to pay for the sins of all of us – anybody of any age.

When Jesus Christ stretched out His arms and died for us on a cross, He was wrapping those arms of love around all of us. The third day He arose. Since He paid for the sins of all of us, no one is excluded from His free offer of eternal life. If we will come as sinners and place our trust in Christ alone to save us, God will give anyone anywhere His free gift of eternal life.

If you are a child, God is saying "Come." If you are of old age, God is saying "Come." If you are middle aged, God is saying, "Come." And to everyone else, God is saying, "Come." Whoever you are, "Come" and put your trust in Christ alone to save you.

5

Come to Christ and You Will Get Two for the Price of One

(using Titus 2:11-13)

Who doesn't like getting two for the price of one? Like when a shoe store says, "Buy one pair, get the second one free."

That is what happens when a person trusts Christ as his or her personal Savior. That two-for-one offer is spoken of in Titus 2:11-13. There we read, "For the grace of God that brings salvation has appeared to all men, teaching us that denying ungodliness and worldly lusts, we should live soberly, righteously, and godly in the present age."

You, first of all, receive *the grace that saves you.* "Grace" means favor given to those who deserve the opposite. The only thing we *deserve* from God is to be separated from Him forever because of our sin. But God extended favor to those who deserve the opposite, by letting His perfect Son die on a cross as our substitute and rise again the third day. If we will accept what His Son did for us, by trusting Christ as our only way to heaven, God will give us the free gift of eternal life. When you come to Christ, you receive the grace that saves you.

But – you get two for the price of one. You not only get the grace that saves you, but through the price of Christ's death on the cross, you get the *grace that trains you.* That grace shows you how to take out of your life what should not be there and put in what should be there.

It teaches you, as the Bible says, how to deny ungodliness and worldly lusts – the things that dishonor God. Instead, it teaches you how to live *soberly* – how to control your passions instead of letting them control you. How to live *righteously* – how to do the right things even when no one is looking. And it teaches you how to live *godly* – how to live in reverence and respect for the One who saved you.

Two for the price of one. When you trust Christ to save you, through His death and resurrection you receive the grace that saves you and the grace that trains you. Because of that grace, you will not only know that you have entered the Christian life, but you will also learn how to live it. Two for the price of one. Today is the day you ought to receive His generous offer.

6

Come to God and You Will Meet the Promise-Keeper, Not the Promise-Breaker
(using Isaiah 7:14, Matthew 1:22-23, John 6:47)

Are you tired of people who break their promises?

Stores promise a full refund if you are not satisfied with their product. Then as you try to return it, you discover there are "conditions" that make that promise invalid. A family member had a mate promise "till death do we part" and then discovered there was someone else he or she found more attractive. Minor or major, promise-breakers are upsetting.

That is one reason you need to have a personal relationship with the Almighty God. He is a promise-keeper not a promise-breaker. One of the greatest promises He ever made and kept impacts your eternal destiny.

That promise is found in Isaiah 7:14. There we are told, "Therefore the Lord Himself will give you a sign: Behold, the virgin shall conceive and bear a Son, and shall call His name Immanuel." The Almighty God promised that He would take a woman of marriageable age who was a virgin and through the Holy Spirit conceive a child who was Immanuel, meaning "God with us."

More than 700 years later in His perfect timing, God kept that promise. Matthew 1:22-23 says about the birth of Jesus Christ, "So all this was done that it might be fulfilled which was spoken by the Lord through the prophet, saying, 'Behold, the virgin shall be with child, and bear a Son, and they shall call His name Immanuel,' which is translated, 'God with us'."

Why did God make and keep that promise? As the Almighty God, He had to punish sin and that punishment is death. But God kept His promise through Mary and brought Jesus Christ into the world to save us from our sin. He allowed that Son to take our punishment and die on a cross as our substitute. The third day Jesus Christ arose from the grave.

Our sin being punished, God can now forgive us and extend to us His free gift of eternal life. All we need to do is accept that gift by trusting Jesus Christ as our personal Savior. He then promises you in John 6:47, "He who believes in Me has everlasting life."

God is a promise-keeper, not a promise-breaker. Will you receive the results of that promise by trusting Christ to save you?

7

Do vs. Done
(using John 19:30)

When we think of what is required to get to heaven, most of us think of one word – do. We immediately think of things we have to do to be accepted by God. *Do* go to church. *Do* love your neighbor. *Do* take the sacraments. *Do* keep the commandments. *Do* get baptized. Part of the reason is because that is how we earn anything on this earth. We have to do something. But we can easily miss that the message of Christianity doesn't center around the two-letter word "*do*," but the four-letter word "*done*."

When Jesus Christ, God's perfect Son, died on a cross two thousand years ago, He said, "It is finished!" That word 'finished' comes from a Greek word that means, "paid in full."

All of us stand before a holy God with a debt of sin. That debt must be paid. Since the punishment for sin is death, every single one of us is sentenced to die and be forever separated from God. But instead of us paying the price for our own sins, Jesus Christ paid for those sins by dying as our substitute. He took the punishment we deserved. When He proclaimed, "It is finished," He was saying, "I have paid your debt in full." He did not make the down payment for our sins—He made the payment in full. When He arose on the third day, that was the seal of approval that God had accepted what His Son had done on our behalf.

That is why you cannot get to heaven by going to church, living a good life, being baptized, or keeping the commandments.

The debt for your sin and mine has already been paid. It is not about what you have to do, but about what Jesus Christ has *already* done. Because the debt has been paid, you must receive eternal life as a *free gift*, by trusting Christ alone to save you. Notice I said Christ *alone*, not Christ *plus* your good life or plus your church attendance. Again, He did not make the down payment: your sins and mine were paid in full.

So, if you want to live forever with God, don't focus on what you have to do. Focus instead on what He has already done and trust in Christ alone to save you.

8

Do Yourself a Favor

(using Romans 1:4)

Have you ever wondered, "Is Jesus Christ the one He said He was?" If not, you should.

After all, more than 60 people have walked the earth claiming to be the Messiah. How do we know if Jesus Christ was the one He said He was or if He was just some imposter trying to deceive the minds of many?

The answer is: it all stands or falls on the resurrection. Romans 1:4 describes Jesus Christ by saying that He was "declared to be the Son of God with power according to the Spirit of holiness, by the resurrection from the dead." That word "declared" means that through His resurrection, Jesus Christ was proven to be the one He said He was – the Son of God, the Savior of the world.

If you have any question that Jesus Christ was the one He said He was, do yourself a favor. Study the evidence behind the resurrection. A British agnostic said it well: "Let's not talk about the other miracles. Let's talk about the resurrection. If the resurrection is true, every other miracle is true. If the resurrection is not true, no other miracle matters."

You might say, "But the Bible is the only book that talks about the resurrection." Not true – it's actually one of the most proven facts of history! Thomas Arnold was a respected scholar and even wrote a three-volume history of Rome. He once said, "I know of no one fact in the history of mankind which is proved by better and fuller evidence of every sort to the understanding of a fair enquirer than that Christ died and rose again from the dead."

The resurrection designates Him to be who He said He was—the Son of God—sent to be the Savior of the world.

His method of saving the world was to take the punishment for sin that you and I deserved, and to die in our place. His resurrection on the third day proved that He had conquered both sin and the grave. Through personal trust in Christ, *the* Savior becomes *our* Savior, and we receive His free gift of eternal life.

So, go ahead. Do yourself a favor. Study the empty tomb. It may cause you to come to that point where you say as many others have, "My Lord and my God!"

9

Don't Put Off until Tomorrow What You Should Do Today

(using James 4:13-14)

Often when we think of our need for a Savior, we say to ourselves, "I plan to come to Christ. I just don't have time to think about that right now." We are sincere. But God gives a warning which we overlook: tomorrow may never come. That is why the time to come to Christ is now, not later.

James 4:13-14 of the Bible tells us, "Come now, you who say, 'Today or tomorrow we will go to such and such a city, spend a year there, buy and sell, and make a profit'; whereas you do not know what will happen tomorrow. For what is your life? It is even a vapor that appears for a little time and then vanishes away." James rebuked the people of his day because they were so confident in their plans that they had decided where they were going to go, what business they would undertake, how long they would be there, and even how much they would make. He had to remind them that no one is promised tomorrow. He compared our lives to a vapor that quickly disappears. Almost every person who has died felt he had at least one more day, one more month, one more year. That tomorrow never came.

God is asking us to recognize that we are sinners, and as sinners we deserve eternal separation from God – *that's* the price for sin! But Jesus Christ, God's perfect Son, *paid* for that sin by dying in our place on a cross. They crucified Him where they should have crucified you and me. The third day He arose victorious over the grave. The price for our sin now paid, God can forgive us of everything wrong we have ever done or will do and give us the gift of eternal life, entirely for free. All we have to do is place our trust in Christ alone to save us. The Bible's promise in John 6:47 is, "He who believes in Me has everlasting life."

But that decision must be made before you die. It can't be made afterwards. Don't be misguided by the thought that there will always be a tomorrow. That tomorrow may never come. Don't put off until tomorrow what you should do today.

10

Don't Worry about Parts of the Bible You Don't Understand; Worry about Those You Do
(using Ephesians 2:8-9)

Some parts of the Bible are difficult to understand. We may have read them ten times and are still uncertain what they mean. Or we feel like we are reading mail meant for someone else.

In moments like those, we'd be wise to remember a quote often attributed to Mark Twain: "I have always noticed that the passages of Scripture which trouble me most are those which I do understand." Although some things in the Bible might be confusing, there are parts of the Bible that could not be stated any clearer.

Take Ephesians 2:8-9 for example. There we are told, "For by grace you have been saved through faith, and that not of yourselves; it is the gift of God, not of works, lest anyone should boast."

We often think that in order to get to heaven we have to go to church, live a good life, keep the Ten Commandments, love our neighbor, be baptized, keep the sacraments—the list could go on. But notice what those two verses say. We are told, it is "the gift of God, not of works." You cannot work your way to heaven. Instead, you have to receive eternal life as a free gift. That is why the sentence continues, "lest anyone should boast." If you could get to heaven by your own efforts, you could brag "I made it!" But those who get to heaven will not be bragging about what they have done for Christ. They will be bragging about what He did for them.

Those two verses say, "By grace you have been saved." "Grace" is favor to those who deserve the opposite. As sinners, all of us were facing eternal separation from God. But God gave us favor we did not deserve by letting His Son take our punishment, die in our place on a cross, and arise the third day. The price of our sin being paid, we can now be saved through what those two verses call "faith" – that means trusting Christ alone to save us.

Those verses could not say it any clearer. It is through Christ we are saved, not our works. Don't worry about the verses you don't understand; worry about those you do. Then ask yourself, "Have I trusted Christ to save me?"

11

Every Marriage Needs a Third Person – of the Right Kind

(using Genesis 2:24, Ephesians 5:33)

A third person in a marriage destroys the marriage bond. It has happened millions of times, and it may sound too familiar for some of you personally. The commitment "till death do we part" is forsaken as someone else comes on the scene.

Yet, every marriage needs a third person - of the right kind. That person has to be Jesus Christ. God is the one that instituted marriage and He is the only one who knows how to make it work. He declared in Genesis 2:24, "Therefore shall a man leave his father and mother and be joined to his wife, and they shall become one flesh." With that in mind, we are told in Ephesians 5:33, "Let each one of you in particular so love his own wife as himself, and let the wife see that she respects her husband."

God wants to show every husband and wife how to do that. He has done that for countless marriages: He can do it for yours. That's why it is important to understand that before there can be a proper relationship with your spouse, there has to a be proper relationship between you and God. In that relationship He can speak to you and you can speak to Him.

You don't have a relationship with God by going to church, living a good life, taking the sacraments, or being baptized. You have to begin by admitting why you *don't* have a relationship with God. It is because you have sinned. That sin has consequences.

Those consequences are death and eternal separation from God.

But God demonstrated how much He loved you by allowing His perfect Son Jesus Christ to die in your place on a cross. He took the punishment that should have been yours, died as your substitute, and rose again. God now asks you to believe - to trust in Jesus Christ as your only way to heaven.

The second you do, you have relationship with Him that can never be broken. Within that relationship, God can now teach you how to love and respect one another, because no one wants to see your marriage work more than He does.

Have you invited that third person into your marriage? In other words, have you trusted Christ as your personal Savior?

12

God Actually is Unfair

(using 2 Corinthians 5:21)

Many accuse God of being unfair. They see good people suffer and wicked people prosper. They see those with a caring spirit having one physical hardship after another while those who live only for themselves live healthy lives. They wonder whose side God is actually on.

What I say may surprise you. God actually is unfair. If you are going to understand the character of God, then you have to understand the most unfair thing God ever did.

It's talked about in 2 Corinthians 5:21. There we read, "For He made Him who knew no sin to be sin for us, that we might become the righteousness of God in Him."

God took His Son who knew no sin and treated Him like a sinner, so He could treat sinners as though they had never sinned. Humanly speaking, that is completely unfair. But God did not act on the basis of fairness; He acted on the basis of love.

We are sinners. We have broken God's commandments, and the punishment for sin is death and eternal separation from God. But God knew He could forgive us if someone who was absolutely perfect would take our punishment. So, God allowed His Son who knew no sin to be sin *for us*. God punished Him where He should have punished us. On the third day, that Son arose from the grave victorious over sin and death. When we trust Him as our Savior, God looks at our sins as paid for by the blood His Son shed on a cross and we are what the Bible calls, "the righteousness of God in Him."

When we trust Christ, God so clothes us with His righteousness that when God looks upon us, He no longer sees our sin. All He sees is the perfection of His Son. We are forever accepted by God not on the basis of what we have done, but on the basis of what God's Son did when He died in our place.

If we accuse God of being unfair, we have to *start* with the cross. God took His perfect Son and treated Him like a sinner, so He could treat sinners as though they had never sinned.

So, the next time you think God is unfair, be thankful that He was. Then receive the free gift of God's unfairness by trusting Jesus as your Savior.

13

God Has a Reputation for Making Miracles out of Messes
(using 1 Corinthians 6:9-11)

Have you ever looked at the resumes of people that God says will one day walk the streets of heaven? It is an impressive list. They are mentioned in 1 Corinthians 6:9-11.

Brace yourself for how God refers to them. He mentions ten classifications of people, a few of whom you might not want as your neighbor.

He calls them fornicators, idolaters, adulterers, homosexuals, sodomites (those that will go so far as to practice sex with an animal), thieves, covetous, drunkards, revilers (those who are verbally abusive), and extortioners (those who criminally try to obtain someone's money or property). The one thing you can say about all of them is that they made a mess out of their lives.

So why are they in heaven? God explains in verse 11, "And such were some of you. But you were *washed* "– that means cleansed by the blood that Jesus Christ shed on a cross when He paid for their sins by dying in their place, taking the punishment they deserved. He died as our substitute and rose again the third day. Then He says, "you were sanctified" – that means set apart to live a new kind of life that would glorify God. Then He continues, "you were *justified*" – that means declared righteous in the sight of God. In other words, each of those people saw themselves as sinners who deserved to be separated from God forever. But they came to God recognizing that Jesus Christ had taken their punishment and they did what God asks them to do – place their trust in Christ alone as their only way to a right standing with God. The moment they did, God declared them righteous in His sight.

With every one of these people God made a miracle out of a mess – something He wants to do for you. We all bring Him different messes, various ways we have ruined our lives. We may not have stolen anything, but we have lied, cheated, hated others, and have had wrong thoughts. Before a holy God we are all a mess.

Today God wants to do what He has a reputation of doing – make a miracle out of a mess. All you have to do is let Him by trusting Christ as your Savior. Will you?

14

God's Greatest Desire for Your Life

(using John 6:40, 5:39)

Have you ever had that nagging question in your mind? Something you think about from the time you crawl out of bed in the morning to the time you fall into bed at night. It is a question you have thought about, dismissed from your mind, then thought about again.

That question is, "What does God really want of me? What does He want me to say or do? What is His desire of me?" You may contemplate everything from what He wants you to do on Sunday, how or where He wants you to live, or where He wants you to work. But what God desires of each of us concerns something far more important.

The Scriptures tell us how God Himself would answer that question, because it was God's own Son Jesus Christ who answered it.

Jesus said in John 6:40, "And this is the will of Him who sent Me, that everyone who sees the Son and believes in Him may have everlasting life; and I will raise him up at the last day." Above everything else, God's desire for each of us is to have everlasting life, so that one day we will be raised up to live with Him forever.

But how do we get that everlasting life? Jesus explained it was for those who "see the Son and believe in Him."

Today, the way we see the Son is through the Scriptures.

Jesus Himself said in John 5:39, "You search the Scriptures, for in them you think you have eternal life; and these are they which testify of Me."

It is through the Scriptures we see Jesus Christ as the One sent by God to take the punishment for sin that we deserved and die as our substitute. The third day He arose from the grave, having conquered both sin and death.

Then, we have to believe. "Believe" means accepting the truth that Christ died for us – we have to trust in Christ alone as our only way to eternal life. Eternal life is not obtained by going to church, being baptized, living a good life, or keeping the commandments. It is the desire of God that you, as a sinner, will place your trust in Christ alone to save you.

What about you? Have you responded to God's desire for you by trusting Christ?

15

God's Love is Not "Iffy"
(using Romans 8:38-39)

Ever meet those who say, "I love you!" only to find out what they really mean is, "I love you *if*"? "I love you... as long as you don't disappoint me." "I love you... as long as you don't do anything shameful or embarrassing." "I love you... as long as what you did to me never happens again." "I love you ...if you love me in return."

That is why if you have never met the Savior, you need to – today! His love never has been and never will be iffy. When He says, "I love you," He means I love you *period*, not I love you *if*. His love is not conditional on your behavior, lifestyle, personality, strengths, weaknesses, income, reputation in the community, prayer life, or Bible study.

In Romans 8:38-39, we are told, "For I am persuaded that neither death nor life, nor angels nor principalities nor powers, nor things present nor things to come, nor height nor depth, nor any other created thing, shall be able to separate us from the love of God which is in Christ Jesus our Lord." Paul the apostle could not have been any more descriptive in explaining how secure we are in Christ. There is nothing we face in life that does not fall under one of those ten categories – death, life, angels, principalities, powers, things present, things to come, height, depth, any created being. There is absolutely no person or thing that can ever separate us from God. Even if we were to come to Christ and one day turn our back on Him, God under no conditions will turn His back on us. Others may say, "I love you if." God says, "I love you period."

Nowhere was that love more clearly demonstrated than two thousand years ago when Jesus Christ died on a cross for our sins. He took the punishment we deserved, died as our substitute, and rose again. If we will receive that love by admitting we are sinners, acknowledging that His Son died in our place and place our trust in Christ alone to save us, at that moment we become a child of God — forever. No one and nothing can sever that relationship.

Maybe you've never known that kind of unconditional love. Want it? Meet Jesus Christ the Savior – the one whose love never has been and never will be "iffy."

16

Hope So or Know So Salvation
(using 1 John 5:13)

If you took a poll on the street and asked your average person, "Do you think you are going to heaven?" most would say, "I hope so." Some may even say, "I am trying to do what is right, I have lived a pretty good life. So, yes, I think so."

It might surprise you to know that not once does Bible talk about an "I hope so" or "I think so" salvation. Instead, the Bible talks about an "I know so" salvation. In 1 John 5:13, you find this statement, "These things I have written to you who believe in the name of the Son of God, that you may know that you have eternal life." The word "know" there means to know absolutely – like you know how many fingers are on your right hand, what your address is, or how old you are. You should be just as certain that if you were to die right now, you would go to heaven.

How can you have that certainty? You might think, "Don't I have to wait until I die and see if my good deeds outweigh the bad?" No, because knowing you are going to heaven is not based on anything you have done, but on something Jesus Christ did for you.

We are all sinners who deserve to be separated from God forever. God's perfect Son Jesus Christ came into the world, and He took the sin that should have caused our death, and actually died in our place. He took our punishment and rose again. By dying in our place, He satisfied the demands of a holy God against everything wrong we have done. God can now accept us, not based on what we have done but based on what Jesus Christ did when He died in our place. We have to simply accept what He did by believing, by placing our trust in Christ alone to save us.

The moment we trust Christ as our only way to eternal life, we are as certain of heaven as though we are already there. Remember 1 John 5:13 says to those who believe, "that you may *know* you have eternal life."

If your life were to end today, do *you* know that you are going to heaven? Come to Christ and you can know you are going to heaven, not hope so.

17

It's Your Move

(using John 1:11-12)

How many times have you played a board game with a bunch of people, and as you took turns going around the table someone overlooked that it was now his or her turn? So, you said to that person, "It's your move."

That is the way it is with God's plan of salvation. God has already made His move. Now it's your turn to make yours.

John 1:11-12 tells us, "He came to His own, and His own did not receive Him. But as many as received Him, to them He gave the right to become children of God, to those who believe in His name."

The Gospel of John tells of how Christ came to the Jewish people and offered Himself as their Messiah. Many rejected Him. To those who did receive Him, He extended His free gift of eternal life. They became what the Bible calls "children of God."

Today Jesus Christ is offering Himself to everybody everywhere. He offers Himself to each and every one of us. Christ took the punishment *we* deserved for the sins *we* committed and died as our substitute. The third day He arose from the grave. God has made His move. He did the *one thing* necessary for us to be forgiven and live with Him forever — He died in our place.

But now it is our move. We have to do what John 1:12 calls "receiving" Him by "believing in His Name." That means we have to come to God as sinners and recognize that Jesus Christ was the One He said He was, that He was God's Son sent by God to take the punishment for our sins and rise again. Since Christ's death is the only basis by which we can be accepted by God, we have to *trust* in Christ alone to save us.

That is why it is now your move. You can reject Him, and God will have no choice but to make you pay for your own sins in eternal separation from Himself. Or you can receive Him by trusting His Son as your personal Savior, forever becoming a child of God.

God has made His move. Now it is your turn to make yours. What move are you going to make? Make the move millions have made – trust Jesus Christ to save you.

18

Mislabeling Can Be Dangerous
(using Genesis 6:5-8)

Mislabeling something can be dangerous, even fatal. Labeling a bottle of painkillers as vitamins may cause a person to take too many. Replacing a "dead end" sign at the end of a highway with a "resume speed" sign could cause a fatal crash. Calling a piece of dynamite, a mere fire-starter does not change its explosive nature.

It is the same with sin. We tend to mislabel it and call it a weakness, mistake, error, mess up, flaw, or blunder. That label may soften it in our eyes, but it doesn't change how serious it really is.

Shortly after God made man, man rebelled against his creator. God minces no words in describing that rebellion. In so doing, you get a picture of how He feels about sin.

We are told in Genesis 6:5-6, "Then the Lord saw that the wickedness of man was great in the earth, and that every intent of the thoughts of his heart was only evil continually. And the Lord was sorry that He had made man on the earth, and He was grieved in His heart." The depth of God's grief is expressed one verse later, "So the Lord said, 'I will destroy man whom I have created from the face of the earth, both man and beast, creeping thing and birds of the air, for I am sorry that I made them'."

Thankfully, the story does not end there. It continues, "But Noah found grace in the eyes of the Lord." Through Noah and his family, God preserved the human race when a flood came upon the entire earth.

You and I have also experienced God's grace. That grace came to us through Jesus Christ. "Grace" means favor to those who deserve the opposite. Because of our sin and how much it grieves the heart of God, sin must be punished. That punishment is death and eternal separation from God in what the Bible calls hell. But God allowed His perfect Son Jesus Christ to take our punishment, die on a cross as our substitute, and arise the third day. Our sin being punished, God can now extend pardon to us if we place our trust in Christ as our only way to heaven.

There is one condition. We must call sin – sin, and not attempt to downplay or mislabel it. It's calling sin what it is and receiving His grace by trusting Christ that puts us in a right standing in God's sight.

19

Nothing Is Worth Being Separated from God Over

(using Mark 9:43-48)

Some things Jesus Christ said sounded severe. But He spoke so directly because He loved so deeply.

In Mark 9, you have one of the harshest sounding paragraphs of the entire Bible. Jesus made these statements. "If your hand causes you to sin, cut it off. It is better for you to enter into life maimed, rather than having two hands, to go to hell, into the fire that shall never be quenched." "If your foot causes you to sin, cut it off. It is better for you to enter life lame, rather than having two feet, to be cast into hell, into the fire that shall never be quenched." "And if your eye causes you to sin, pluck it out. It is better for you to enter the kingdom of God with one eye, rather than having two eyes, to be cast into hell fire."

Jesus was not suggesting a careless mutilation of the body. His point was that nothing is worth being separated from God over. If the things our hands are touching, the places our feet are taking us, or what our eyes are seeing are keeping us from recognizing our need for Christ, we would be doing ourselves a favor to cut off the hand, cut off the foot, or pluck out the eye. It is better to be here with one of each than separated from God forever with two.

That's why, until you come to Christ, nothing else matters. Don't allow anything to distract you from your need of Christ.

But coming to Christ does not mean finding the right church to attend, doing a certain amount of good deeds, being baptized, or even cleaning up your act. It means acknowledging that you are a sinner deserving of eternal separation from God—but that Jesus Christ died for you on a cross taking the punishment you deserved and rose again. By substituting His life for yours, He bridged the gap of separation between you and God. Coming to God as a sinner, you place your trust in Christ as Savior and receive His free gift of eternal life. Jesus' promise is, "He who believes in Me has everlasting life."

Until that is settled, nothing else matters. Nothing is worth being separated from God over. Don't let anything keep you from recognizing your need for Christ.

20

One Gift You Can Never Lose
(using John 10:28)

Think of a gift you have received that you thought, "I don't know what I would do if I ever lost that."

It could be a piece of jewelry, a hand-me-down from a relative, something a friend gave that means nothing to anybody else but everything to you, a certificate worth $1000 in savings, or the paper deed that is the only proof a property is yours. The fear of losing that gift sparks dread and panic.

God has a gift He would like to give us. Not only is it the most valuable gift you will ever receive, it is completely free. But on top of it all, there is no way you could ever lose it.

That gift is eternal life. Jesus said in John 10:28, "And I give them eternal life, and they shall never perish; neither shall anyone snatch them out of My hand."

It is the most *valuable* gift because there is nothing greater than knowing that you will live in God's presence forever – no sickness, no sorrow, no pain, no problems. There is not a single thing that God could give us that would mean more than that.

It's *free* because the price for that gift has already been paid. The price of sin is death and eternal separation from God. But Jesus Christ paid that price when He came into the world and offered Himself as sacrifice. He took the punishment that we as sinners deserved and died on a cross in our place. The third day He arose. Since the price for sin has been paid, God can offer eternal life free to anyone anywhere. We receive that gift by believing – by trusting in Christ alone as our only way to eternal life.

But the best news of all is that you can never lose that gift. Jesus emphatically declared, "and they shall *never* perish, neither shall *anyone* snatch them out of my hand." God never takes back that gift, and nobody can take that gift from us. To do so, they would have to be greater than God Himself.

Receive His gift of eternal life and you are guaranteed by God Himself that you will never lose that gift. To belong to Him is to belong to Him forever.

21

One Question the Bible Answers Clearly

(using Job 14:14, John 11:25-26, 14:19)

There are numerous questions the Bible never answers, much to our frustration.

Why do good people suffer? Why do those who do evil and even harm others go unpunished? Why doesn't a loving God stop natural catastrophes that kill thousands?

But there is one question the Bible not only asks, but answers *clearly.* It is a question raised by a person named Job in the Old Testament and one that you may have asked.

In Job 14:14, Job asks, "If a man dies, shall he live again?" In context, Job has gone through so much hardship, his suffering and eventual death causes him to raise that question.

Jesus Christ answered that question with an emphatic "yes" when His friend Lazarus died. Christ said in John 11:25-26, "I am the resurrection and the life. He who believes in Me, though he may die, he shall live. And whoever lives and believes in Me shall never die." Never! Imagine that!

You might ask, "How do we know He's right?" The answer is because Jesus Christ arose from the grave. His resurrection *guarantees* yours. In John 14:19 Jesus said, "Because I live, you will live also."

The resurrection of Jesus Christ from the grave is a fact that nobody has been able to disprove even though many have tried. Frank Morison, who wrote *Who Moved the Stone* became a believer after trying to disprove the resurrection. That resurrection is what proved that Christ had conquered your sin and mine. Since He died as our substitute, taking the punishment for sin we deserved, His resurrection on the third day guarantees that those who believe in Him will experience that same victory. When their eyes close here, they open in the presence of the Lord.

That word "believe" means to trust, depend, rely on. Coming to God as a sinner and recognizing that Jesus Christ died in your place and rose again, you have to trust in Christ alone as your only way to eternal life. When you trust Christ as your personal Savior, your resurrection is as certain as His. Instead of being separated from Him for eternity, you will live in His presence forever.

To the question, "If a man dies, shall he live again?" God doesn't just answer, "Yes." He *shouts,* "Yes! Yes! Yes!" If you will trust Him to save you, His resurrection guarantees yours.

22

Only Jesus Christ Can Break Your Chains
(using John 8:36)

Some of us have tried everything. Counseling, prescription medication, accountability, and a host of other remedies. Yet we cannot seem to break the chains of alcoholism, drugs, sexual temptation, pornography, and uncontrolled anger.

Why? It's because we have not gone to someone who is powerful enough to help us say "yes" to things we should say yes to and "no" to things we should say no to. Referring to Jesus Christ, John 8:36 of the Bible says, "Therefore if the Son makes you free, you shall be free indeed."

How can He help? God so hates sin that the punishment for sin is death. But He also loves us, so Jesus Christ came into the world and suffered death in our place. He died on the cross taking the punishment that we deserved and died as our substitute. When He arose the third day, that was proof of His victory over sin and the grave. His death and resurrection are the only means by which you can be right before God.

When you trust Jesus Christ as your Savior, the same power that brought Christ out of the grave dwells within you. That is why the Bible says, "Therefore if the Son makes you free, you can be free indeed." You no longer have to surrender to the temptations and vices you once did. Some believers get victory quickly. For others it takes time, with some struggles along the way. But with

Christ in our lives, the process of growth definitely begins. You have a Person and power to live a life of victory instead of defeat. You can say "no" to temptation instead of "yes." You can be a victor instead of a victim.

How do you receive Jesus Christ and experience that victory? You do it by faith – by what the Bible calls "believing." It's trust in Jesus Christ who died for you as your only way to eternal life, your only way to be free from the bondage of sin. You have to trust Him as your personal Savior. When you do, the chains that used to bind you lose their grip. Victory may not come overnight, but through His presence and power in your life, it will come.

Don't try to free yourself from whatever has you in chains. It will never happen. Come to Christ and meet the chain-breaker.

23

Salvation is Not Christ Plus, but Christ Period
(using John 6:47)

Try it sometime. Ask a person on the street, "What do you think you have to do to get to heaven?" Oftentimes, the answer will be – come to Christ and then live a good life. Or, come to Christ and be baptized. Come to Christ and go to church. Come to Christ and keep the Ten Commandments. Come to Christ and take the sacraments. The problem with all those is that we are putting a comma where God puts a period.

John 6:47 contains one of the simplest sentences in the entire Bible. Jesus Himself said, "Most assuredly I say to you, he who believes in Me has everlasting life." Make sure to notice that He did *not* say "He who believes in Me, *comma*, and lives a good life." He did not say "He who believes in Me, *comma*, and goes to church." He did not say "He who believes in Me, *comma*, and is baptized." What He said is followed by a period, not a comma. He who believes in Me has everlasting life – **period**.

The reason is, in order to have eternal life you have to be satisfied with the thing that satisfied God. When Christ died on a cross, He said, "It is finished." That word finished means "paid in full." Jesus Christ made complete payment for our sins and did everything necessary for us to receive eternal life. His resurrection the third day proved God accepted His Son's death as complete and total payment for our sins.

God was not satisfied with His Son's death *and* your good works. He was not satisfied with His Son's death *and* your church attendance. He was not satisfied with Son's death *and* your baptism. He was only satisfied with the fact that His Son died for you.

That is why you have to come to God and do what the Bible calls "believe" – that means trust in Christ alone to save you. As you depend on a chair to hold your weight, or a doctor to treat you, you have to place your trust in Christ alone as your only way to heaven. It's not Christ plus something you have done that saves you, but Christ period.

Don't put a comma where God puts a period. Trust in Christ alone as your only way to heaven. Salvation is not Christ *plus*, but Christ *period*.

24

Satan's Primary Goal in Your Life

(using 2 Corinthians 4:3-4)

The Devil, called Satan in the Bible, is alive and well on planet Earth. There are many things he loves to do in people's lives. But the thing that he most enjoys is the very thing that could damage you the greatest. It could cause you to spend an eternity separated from God. In short, Satan wants to keep you out of heaven.

What I am referring to is what Paul the apostle speaks of in 2 Corinthians 4:3-4 of the New Testament. Paul uses these words: "But even if our gospel is veiled, it is veiled to those who are perishing, whose minds the god of this age has blinded, who do not believe, lest the light of the gospel of the glory of Christ, who is the image of God, should shine on them."

Satan has blindfolded you. He prefers that you not understand that Jesus Christ, God's perfect Son, is the image of God Himself, who is able to do for us what no one else can do.

As humans created by God, we had fallen away from God through sin. Nothing we do ourselves could restore our relationship with God. But Jesus Christ made it possible for that relationship to be restored by dying on a cross and paying the price *our* sins deserved. That Son is alive today because He arose from the grave on the third day.

What Satan doesn't want you to know is that when we as sinners trust Christ as our personal Savior, the only One who could restore our relationship with God, we are forever His. That's what happens when we believe what God calls the gospel – the good news of Jesus Christ.

Satan wants you to remain blind to the fact that your relationship with God can be restored today. In an endeavor to keep you blinded, he will use all kinds of lies and deception. Because Satan knows if you reject Christ you will spend eternity the same place Satan himself is going to spend it - separated from God forever. He would prefer that you believe lies such as 'Jesus Christ was not actually the Son of God' or, 'There is no God. When we die, we all go to the same place. A good life will get you to heaven.'

Don't let Satan blind you any longer. Receive the good news of Jesus Christ and trust Him today as your Savior.

25

Satisfaction is Found in a Person, not Possessions

(using Ecclesiastes 2:10-11, John 6:35)

Go to any thesaurus on your bookshelf or online. Look up the word "satisfaction." and you will find the synonyms fulfillment, pleasure, contentment, happiness, comfort. All of us would agree that those are good synonyms for satisfaction. The question is, where do you find true satisfaction?

In the Bible, King Solomon—one of the wisest people who ever lived—tells us where satisfaction is *not* found. In terms of material possession and life's comforts, Solomon had it all. Wealth, power, fame, influence – you name it, he had it.

That is what makes his words in Ecclesiastes 2:10-11 so alarming. He says, "Whatever my eyes desired I did not keep from them. I did not withhold my heart from any pleasure, for my heart rejoiced in all my labor; and this was my reward from all my labor. Then I looked on all the works my hands had done and on the labor in which I had toiled; and indeed all was vanity and grasping for the wind. There was no profit under the sun." After all he had done and experienced, he never found satisfaction.

The reason? Because possessions and everything that goes with them will only meet our physical needs temporarily. Satisfaction comes when our *spiritual* needs are met. That's why Jesus said in John 6:35, "I am the bread of life. He who comes to Me shall never hunger, and he who believes in Me shall never thirst." When He used the term Bread of Life, he meant the bread that supplies life. Physical bread will supply your physical needs. He was saying, "I, and I alone, am the one who can meet your spiritual needs."

When you come to Christ, you not only find life here on earth in terms of a satisfaction that cannot be bought, but eternal life in the presence of God Himself – something that cannot be bought with mere *things*. Satisfaction is found in a Person, not possessions.

You can have that satisfaction today by coming to God as a sinner, recognizing that Jesus Christ died on a cross in your place and that He took the punishment you deserved, then rose again the third day. You have to trust Him alone as your personal Savior.

So, what are you relying on to satisfy you – something you have or Someone you know?

26

Talk to the Person Who Lives There
(using John 14:2-3,6)

How many times have you wanted to go somewhere and were not sure how to get there? When you need directions, who is the best person to ask? Wouldn't it be a person who actually lives there?

That is why if you want to know how to get to heaven, the best person to talk to is Jesus Christ because He lives there. He once told His disciples that He was going to prepare a place for them, adding, "that where *I am*, there you may be also." One of His disciples, Thomas, basically asked, "But how do we get there?"

Jesus answered in eighteen words. He said, "I am the way, the truth, and the life. No one comes to the Father except through Me." Now please note, Jesus did not say, "I know the way, I know the truth, I know the life." Instead He said, "I *am* the way, I *am* the truth, I *am* the life."

He was saying that salvation is in a person. It is not in a schedule of going to church, a system of doing good deeds, or in a set of sacraments. *Salvation is in a person.* You dare not trust *something* to save you; you must trust *Someone*.

That someone has to be the One who died on a cross for your sins.

Because we are all sinners we deserve to die and be forever separated from God. But God allowed His Son to take your

51

punishment and mine on a cross and rise again the third day. For that reason, you have to come to God as a sinner and place your trust in a Person—Jesus Christ—as your only way to eternal life because He paid for your sins by dying in your place.

When you trust Christ, you have the *way*. He will take you directly to heaven when you die. You have the *truth*, all the truth you need for life and for living. You have the *life* – life that culminates in the presence of God Himself.

Jesus knows how to get to heaven. He lives there. Just come to Christ, trusting Him to save you, and you will be as sure of heaven as though you are already there.

27

The Best Definition and Example of Love
(using 1 John 4:10)

We live in a day when the word love stands for everything from Hollywood to heaven. Sometimes we struggle to know what love really is.

But the best definition and example of love you will ever find is in 1 John 4:10. There we read, *"In this is love,* not that we loved God, but that He loved us and sent His Son to be the propitiation for our sins."

That verse defines love as putting someone else first, even if it means the sacrifice of yourself.

The word propitiation means "satisfaction." There is a God, and He is holy and just. Being the holy God He is, He has to do what is right and punish sin. That is why in order for us to live forever with God, His justifiable anger against our sin had to be satisfied, meaning the sin must be punished.

The problem is that you and I cannot take the punishment for each other's sin. We are both sinners. Whoever paid for our sins had to be 100% perfect.

Jesus Christ, God's only Son fulfilled that requirement. Jesus was without sin. There was no reason, humanly speaking, for Him to die. But remember how God defines love through the example of His own Son? Love puts someone else first even if it means the sacrifice of yourself.

The Bible tells us that God loved us so much that He allowed

His perfect Son to die in our place taking the punishment that we deserved. God could have kept Him in heaven and the two of them could have had heaven to themselves. But God expressed His love for us by allowing His Son to die for us.

When Christ arose the third day, that was proof that God accepted what His Son did on our behalf. God can now give us eternal life free, if we will simply believe – that means trust in Christ alone to save us. When we trust Christ as our personal Savior, God no longer has to punish us for our sin because we are accepting what His Son did on our behalf.

When God tells us He loves us, He proved it. He put us first even though it meant the sacrifice of His own Son. Come to Christ. You will meet the One who put you first by sacrificing Himself.

28

The Best is Yet to Come
(using Revelation 21:4-5)

One thing that keeps us from seeing our need for Christ is that we feel like things are going well. We have a good job, a nice home, a nice car, and the family seems happy. "What more do I need?" we are tempted to say.

The problem is that we're overlooking two things. One is the seriousness of sin. Regardless of what we have, we cannot overlook what we have done. We are sinners, and even the smallest sin must be punished.

But Jesus Christ loved us so much that He, as the perfect Son of God, took our punishment and died on our behalf. He died in our place and rose again the third day. Through simple trust in Christ, we can now be forgiven of any and all sin and live in His presence forever.

Nothing we have matters if we don't have Christ. Sin is serious—but so is forgiveness. When we trust Christ to save us, we are forever His.

There is a second thing we are overlooking. That is, the best is yet to some. Absolutely nothing we have now, regardless of its grandeur, comes *close* to what God has for us in heaven. That is undoubtedly one reason the Bible tells us little about heaven. No human mind could ever grasp what heaven is going to be like. It is beyond anything imaginable.

Look at just one thing the Bible says about heaven. In

Revelation 21:4-5 we are told, "'And God will wipe away every tear from their eyes; there shall be no more death, nor sorrow, nor crying. There shall be no more pain, for the former things have passed away.' Then He who sat on the throne said, 'Behold, I make all things new.'"

Don't miss those two words "every" and "all." Every tear or reason for sorrow is removed. Nothing sad, disappointing, or unfortunate happens in heaven. All things are new. Heaven is not a remake of the finest on earth. Everything is brand spanking new – something that has never been seen before. In a word: unfathomable.

That is one reason among thousands that I would beg you to come to Christ today. You will receive eternal forgiveness. But you will also live each day with the exhilaration of knowing the best is yet to come.

29

The Best Way I Can Use My Tongue
(using Proverbs 18:21a)

Have you ever considered how much power is in our tongue? Proverbs 18:21 contains an intriguing phrase. It reads, "Death and life are in the power of the tongue."

The tongue can make two people the best of friends; it can make two people the worst of enemies. The tongue can cause two people to celebrate the uniting of their lives in holy matrimony. The same two tongues can cause them later to walk life apart as they file for divorce. The tongue can start a war; the tongue can stop a war. Whoever wins or loses a presidential election does so by the persuasive use of the tongue. Death and life are in the power of the tongue.

With that in mind I want to use my tongue this morning in the greatest way this tongue could ever be used. In fact, it's the greatest way, if you understand what I am about to tell you, that you can ever use yours. That is to explain to you how you can live forever in the presence of God.

There is one thing keeping that from happening as we sit here right now. That is summed up in a three-letter word called "sin." We have broken God's commandments. We have lied, cheated, hated, stolen, entertained wrong thoughts, and said unkind words. According to God, that sin must be punished by eternal separation from Him in a place the Bible calls hell.

The greatest way I could ever use my tongue is to tell you

that you don't have to spend eternity separated from God. God's perfect Son, Jesus Christ, came into the world and He took your sin and my sin, placed it upon Himself, and died in our place. He was punished where we should have been punished. Three days later Jesus Christ proved his victory over sin and the grave by rising from the dead.

That's why you can enjoy eternal life as a free gift, because the price for your sin has been paid. All you have to do is come to God as a sinner, recognize Jesus Christ died for you and rose again, and place your trust in Christ alone to save you. God's Word says, "He who has the Son has life."

That's the greatest thing my tongue could ever tell you. Trust Christ to save you.

30

The Biggest Difference
Between Religion and Christ
(using Luke 18:9-14)

Confusing two things can cause tremendous damage. Confusing diesel fuel with unleaded gasoline can damage and engine or possibly cause an explosion. Mistaking a one-way with a two-way street can be equally dangerous.

In the spiritual realm, nothing is more dangerous than confusing religion with a relationship with Christ. Such confusion can have eternal consequences. The reason is that religion can take you to church but only Christ can take you to heaven.

No paragraph in the Bible makes that any clearer than Luke 18:9-14 where Christ speaks of two men who—in a manner of speaking—went to "church" one Sunday. They went up to the temple to pray. One was a Pharisee and the other a tax collector. The Pharisee reminded God of the exemplary life, in his opinion, he had lived as well as his religious deeds and devotions. The tax collector, on the other hand, recognized his sinfulness and asked God for mercy. His attitude was, "If you have never met a sinner, meet me — the number one sinner." Referring to the tax collector, Jesus Christ made an interesting declaration. He said, "I tell you, this man went down to his house justified rather than the other."

We, too, need God's mercy. That mercy has already been demonstrated for us when Jesus Christ, God's perfect Son, died for us. On that cross He took the punishment for sin that you and I deserved and became our substitute. The anger of God against our sin was poured out on Christ. He died in our place and rose the third day.

If anything we have done in terms of going to church, helping others, living a good life, being baptized, taking the sacraments, or keeping the Ten Commandments would get us to heaven, then Christ's death would not have been necessary. We have to come to God the way the tax collector did, recognizing we are sinners in need of mercy. Only if we place our trust in Christ alone to save us will God forgive us of our sins and give us His free gift of eternal life.

The Bible is clear. Religion will take you to church, but only Christ can take you to heaven. Whatever you do, don't confuse the two. To receive eternal life, the Bible never says, "Come to church." It always says, "Come to Christ."

31

The Day You Die Ought to be
More Exciting than the Day You Were Born
(using Ecclesiastes 7:1)

Many people were excited the day you were born. So excited, that those close to you celebrate that birthday every year. Have you ever considered that, in many ways, the day you die should be more exciting than the day you were born?

There is an interesting sentence in the Bible that you may have never seen. It only contains eleven words, and can be missed so easily. In Ecclesiastes 7:1 we are told, "A good name is better than precious ointment" and then here are those eleven words "and the day of death than the day of one's birth."

The day you die ought to be more exciting than the day you were born. What a profound thought. But why?

For two reasons. One is, in the context of Ecclesiastes, you have lived your life in a way that your influence will never be forgotten. The book of Ecclesiastes tells us how to develop a skill for living – to live in such a way that you leave a legacy that will remain for generations to come.

The second reason—which is explained clearly throughout Scripture—is that if you know for sure that when you die you will be in the presence of God forever, dying is far more exciting than living. Because you know the moment you are absent from the body, you are what the Bible calls "present with the Lord."

That is why the greatest need every person has is for a

personal relationship with Jesus Christ. First of all, He is the one who fashioned you in your mother's womb. He made you the unique person you are. Since He gave you the abilities you have, He knows how your life can have the greatest influence that you could ever have.

Secondly, Jesus Christ is the only one who can give you eternal life. On the cross two-thousand years ago, Jesus Christ took the punishment for all your sins and rose again the third day. Since the price for your sin had been paid, if you trust Him as your personal Savior, He will give you the free gift of eternal life today.

Come to Christ today. Then let the day you die be more exciting than the day you were born. You will be with Him forever.

32

The Greatest Formula in the Bible
(using John 5:24)

You may be surprised that the Bible contains formulas, things that, if you mix them together, have a certain, set outcome. The greatest formula of the Bible is only six words long. What makes it the greatest formula is that it explains how you can live forever in the presence of God.

That formula is: *hearing plus believing equals eternal life.* The verse I am referring to is John 5:24. There we are told, "Most assuredly, I say to you, he who hears My word and believes in Him who sent Me has everlasting life, and shall not come into judgment, but has passed from death into life."

First, you have to *hear* and understand the Word that Jesus Christ is the Savior of the world. The reason the Bible calls Him the Savior is that we are all what the Bible calls "lost" — sinners facing eternal separation from God. Jesus' method of saving us was to take the punishment sinners deserved and die as their substitute. He was punished where we should have been punished for *our* sins. Three days later He arose victorious over sin and the grave.

... *plus* believing. That means you have to accept what you heard as being true and trust that Jesus' sacrifice saved you — not your church attendance, your good life, your baptism, or anything you've done. You have to trust in Christ alone as your only way to heaven.

The moment someone places his trust in Christ to save him, the Bible says that person *has* eternal life — that means right now. Eternal life is not something you pick up when die. It is something you have the moment you trust Christ to save you.

Then John 5:24 continues, "you shall not come into judgment." That is a promise that cannot be broken by a God who cannot lie. You will never be condemned for your sins.

John 5:24 concludes, "has passed from death into life." Death isn't in front of you; it is behind you. There's no need to fear death anymore. The moment your eyes close here, you are forever in His presence.

When you hear and believe, you have eternal life right now; you will never come into judgment; you have already passed from death into life. *Hearing plus believing equals eternal life.* The greatest formula of the Bible.

Right now, will you hear and believe?

33

The Lord's Table Looks Three Ways
(using 1 Corinthians 11:23-29)

When you eat at the kitchen table at home, you are looking forward. That is, you know that meal is going to sustain you for the next few hours.

Don't confuse the Lord's Table with your kitchen table. To begin with, the Lord's Table is spiritual in nature, not physical. The Lord's Table is all about Him, not you. And rather than just looking *forward*, the Lord's Table looks three ways.

First, it looks backward. Jesus said, "'Take, eat; this is My Body which is broken for you; do this in remembrance of Me.' In the same manner He also took the cup after supper, saying, 'This cup is the new covenant in My blood. This do, as often as you drink it, in remembrance of Me'."

We are looking back at what Christ did on a cross two thousand years when He took the punishment for our sins. He gave His body and blood in our place. The third day He arose from the grave, proving His victory over sin and death. To be right with God, we have to receive what He did for us by admitting we are sinners, believing the truth that Christ died for us, and trust Christ alone to save us.

Second, the Lord's Table looks forward. We are to take part in this memorial and proclaim its purpose until He returns. This memorial is done in anticipation of His coming. Once He comes, there will be no longer be a need for it because those who have trusted Him as their Savior will be forever in His presence.

But the Lord's Table also looks inward. God says, "Whoever eats this bread and drinks this cup of the Lord in an unworthy manner will be guilty of the body and blood of the Lord." That means, the Lord's Table is only for believers, those who have trusted Him as Savior. The Lord's table is not for unbelievers. It's also only for believers who are taking seriously the meaning of what they are doing and are not holding onto unconfessed sin or a wrong and un-Christlike attitude towards others. Participating in the Lord's Table is a serious act of worship, unlike any other table you approach.

So, ask yourself, "Do I qualify to participate in this worship experience? Have I come to Christ, and am I attempting to live a life that honors Him?"

34

The Mark of a True Friend
(using John 8:7)

All of us need a friend. We would agree with the person who said, "Without friends, life is like a rose garden without flowers."

But there are two kinds of friends. There are those who tell us what we want to hear. If we accept what they say, we walk away feeling good. However, the mark of a true friend is that they also tell us what we *need* to hear. If we accept what they say, we walk away knowing we have been helped.

Jesus Christ had a nickname, "Friend of sinners." One of the reasons He was such a true friend is that He always told people what they needed to hear even if it wasn't always what they wanted to hear.

One time a woman was caught in the sin of adultery. Her accusers brought her to Jesus and suggested that she be stoned. But Jesus looked at them as we are told in John 8:7 and said, "He who is without sin among you, let him throw a stone at her first." His reason was simple. Even though they may not have sinned the way she did, they were still sinners. He told them what they needed to hear. They needed to point the finger at themselves.

There are three things Jesus Christ as your true friend wants you to hear. One is that you are a sinner and, being a just God, He cannot overlook that sin. He has to punish it. That punishment is everlasting separation from God in what the Bible calls hell.

But the second thing He wants you to hear is that He has

already paid for that sin. On a cross two thousand years ago, He became our substitute. He allowed Himself to be punished in our place. His resurrection the third day proved that God accepted what His Son did on your behalf.

That is why the third thing God wants you to know is that Christ and Christ *alone* can save you. You have to believe that Christ is your only way to heaven. Your good life or your church attendance will not save you. He, and only He, can save you.

Jesus is a true friend. He tells you what you need to hear. Accept today what that true friend has to say.

35

The Most Humble Person You Will Ever Meet
(using Philippians 2:8)

Humility is rarely one of our strengths. In fact, if I were to ask who the most humble people you know are, that would take more effort than to name the most prideful people you know.

But if you would like to know the greatest example of humility, I know of no better person to suggest than Jesus Christ. The proof is that He did for you and for me something that we wouldn't likely do for another.

Philippians 2:8 speaks of this act of humility when it says, "And being found in appearance as a man, He humbled Himself and became obedient to the point of death, even the death of the cross."

You and I have at least one thing in common. We are both sinners. You sin your way, and I sin my way. That sin must be punished, and that punishment is death. We deserve to die and be forever separated from God. The only way we could be forgiven was if someone was willing to take our place.

Jesus Christ was and is the Son of God. He is *absolutely* perfect – never told a lie, never had an unkind thought. He as the Son of God was the only one who qualified.

So instead of enjoying the grandeur of heaven, He selflessly accepted His Father's will and came to earth for the precise purpose of dying for us. Imagine that! The Creator dying for His creation. Being unequivocally perfect, He could take the punishment for our sin and die in our place.

That death was death on a cross – the most painful and humiliating way a person could die. The cross was the punishment reserved for the worst of thieves and murderers who were deemed to deserve the cruelest death possible. The third day He arose from the grave - proof that God accepted His Son's death as sufficient payment for our sins. Because of His substitutionary death God can now extend eternal life as a free gift to all those who will place their trust in Him alone to save them.

Come to Christ and you will meet the most humble person you have ever known. His death on the cross in *your* place as *your* substitute demonstrated the depth of His humility.

36

The Most Important Word in the Christmas Story

(using Luke 2:11)

With the holiday season approaching you will likely hear the story behind Christmas. You may hear one verse of the Bible quoted more often at this time of the year than any other. It is Luke 2:11 where we are told, "For there is born to you this day in the city of David a Savior, who is Christ the Lord."

Whatever you do, don't miss one word. It's the most important word in the whole story. It is the word "Savior."

Suppose that word was "leader" instead. That would be truthful and encouraging because, indeed, Jesus Christ was that. But we would still be forever separated from God when we die. Suppose that word was the word "teacher." That, too, would be truthful and encouraging. Indeed, Jesus Christ was the greatest teacher of all time. But we would still be forever separated from God when we die. What if that word was "friend"? Once again, that is accurate and encouraging. In fact, His nickname was the "friend of sinners." But we would *still* be separated from God when we die.

Don't miss the one word that makes all the difference. "For there is born to you this day in the city of David, a *Savior...* "

Sin must be punished, and that punishment is death and eternal separation from God. So how did Christ become our Savior?

God, being a holy God, has to punish sin. The only way He could forgive us would be for someone else to take that punishment in our place. That "someone" had to be absolutely perfect. You cannot die for me, nor I for you, because both of us are sinners. We both deserve punishment. Jesus Christ, the *perfect* Son of God became human, was born in a manger, and 33 years later died on a cross as our substitute. He arose from the dead three days later as proof that God had accepted what His Son did on our behalf. God will give you eternal life as a free gift if you will trust Christ as your only way to eternal life. All because when Christ came into the world He came as the Savior.

Let me ask you something – it's the most important question you may be asked this Christmas season. Jesus Christ is the Savior. Has He become *your* Savior?

37

The One Thing that Stands Between You and God

(using Isaiah 59:1-2)

When you're talking to God, does it ever feel like you're talking a brick wall? Nothing ever seems to happen, and you even wonder if He is listening.

There's a chance He is not! Because in every one of our lives there is something that can stand between us and God. Isaiah 59:1-2 tells us what that is. There we read, "Behold, the Lord's hand is not shortened, that it cannot save; nor his ear heavy, that it cannot hear. But your iniquities have separated you from your God; and your sins have hidden His face from you, so that He will not hear."

In context, God is talking to the nation Israel — a nation that had strayed from Him. Their sin was keeping them from the deliverance that only God could give from those who wanted to destroy them. But those words established a basic principle – sin in our lives can keep God from hearing us and working on our behalf.

The reason sin is a barrier is that God's character is perfect and all righteous. A holy God cannot tolerate sin; He has to punish it. A holy God applauds righteousness and punishes sin. Otherwise He would be a hypocrite – a person who says one thing and does another. Our sin is a barrier between ourselves and God.

You cannot remove that sin by buddying up to God by going to church, being good, being baptized, or taking the sacraments. The punishment for sin is death. Someone has to die. That is why, two thousand years ago, there was a death on a cross that has been called the most significant event in history. On that cross, instead of God punishing you for your sin and me for mine, He punished His perfect Son in our place. God hung Him on the cross where He should have hung you and me. The third day that Son came up from the grave, proving that God accepted what Christ did in our place.

God now asks us to believe — to trust in Christ alone as our only way to heaven. The moment we trust Christ, our sin is forgiven. There is no longer a barrier between you and God.

You cannot remove what is standing between you and God. God can and wants to, if you will let Him by trusting Christ today as your personal Savior.

38

The Past Can Be a Memory, Not a Nightmare
(using Acts 10:43)

One thing often keeps us from living in the present and the future. It's called the past. We think of all the things we wish we had never done, all the thoughts we wish we had never had, and all the words we wish we had never spoken. The past becomes a nightmare.

God has an answer. It's called forgiveness. In Acts 10:43, the apostle Peter announced to a man named Cornelius something that the whole world needs to hear when he said, "To Him all the prophets witness that, through His name, whoever believes in Him will receive remission of sins."

That word remission means forgiveness. In other words, God would like to release you from the guilt of everything wrong you have done. God would like to pardon you.

Abraham Lincoln was once asked, "Suppose a man rebelled against you and then came back and said he was sorry. How would you treat that man?" Abraham Lincoln answered, "I would treat him as though he had never done a thing wrong." That is what God means by forgiveness. He would like to treat you as though you have never done anything wrong.

How can He do that? The verse I just mentioned answers that in six words: "that through His Name, whoever believes." That phrase, "through His name," refers to who Christ is and what He did. That means forgiveness is yours on the basis *what Christ did*. Jesus Christ paid for your sins by taking your punishment on a cross. The third day He rose from the grave. Forgiveness is now mine on the basis of *what I do*. "Believe" means you come to God as a sinner and *trust* in Christ alone to save you. The moment you do, God forgives you of everything wrong you *have* ever done or *will* ever do because His Son took your punishment.

You might say, "But it will still be on my mind." Yes, but that's not the problem. The problem is, it's on your conscience. When God forgives you, He takes it from your conscience— and when it comes to your mind, it is simply a memory, not a nightmare, because you realize you have been forgiven.

Come to Christ. Let God put your past where it should be – in the past. It will only be a memory. Not a nightmare.

39

The People You are
Attracted to the Most

(using Luke 19:5-6, John 3:16)

Let me ask you a question. What kind of person are you drawn to the most?

Typically, you are most drawn to the people you know love you. That is why you might feel more drawn -to your mother than you do to your mother-in-law; your mother-in-law loves your spouse, but your mother loves you. That is why you are more attracted to one employer than you are to another; the one employer loved the work that you did, but this employer loves you. It's a fact that we are drawn to the people we know love *us*.

That's why people just like us were so immensely drawn to Jesus Christ. It was not because they loved Him, but they could sense He loved them.

The Bible tells us of Jesus walking through the city of Jericho. A short man named Zacchaeus, despised for his occupation as a tax collector, climbed a tree so that he could see the Lord. When Jesus saw him, He said to him, "Hurry up and come down, for today I must stay at your house." And the Bible tells us that Zacchaeus "received Him joyfully."

Why did so many welcome Jesus with open arms? It was not because they loved Him, but they could sense here was a person who loved them.

The best proof of His love is seen in what happened on a

cross two thousand years ago. Jesus Christ gave Himself as our substitute and took the punishment for sin that we deserved. He died in our place. The third day He arose from the grave. Through personal trust in Christ, we can be forgiven of our sin, and receive the free gift of eternal life. That is why one of the best-known sentences of the Bible - John 3:16 - tells us, "For God so loved the world that He gave His only begotten Son, that whoever believes in Him should not perish but have everlasting life."imHim should not perish but have everlasting lifde."

The more you learn about Christ, the more you will be drawn to Him. Because you are not drawn to the people you love, but to the ones whom you feel love you. Jesus loved you all the way to the grave – and back! Receive that love and come to Him.

40

The Truth Hurts,
But It Also Helps

(using Isaiah 53:6)

"The truth hurts, doesn't it?" It's a familiar phrase. Someone may say, "You're not as prideful as some, but at times you are rather stuck on yourself." Or, "You are not nearly as patient with people as you say you are." A spouse may say, "Why don't you let me finish that project? If it is left up to you, it won't ever get done."

The truth hurts, but it also helps. If you let it, the truth helps you face the facts and do something about them.

Nobody is more truthful with us than God is. So much so, that when He talks about us, guess what He compares us with? Sheep. Not horses, donkeys, dogs, or cats — but *sheep*. We are told in Isaiah 53:6, "All we like sheep have gone astray; we have turned, every one, to his own way; and the Lord has laid on Him the iniquity of us all."

No animal is more prone to wander off than a sheep. It will see a bush and walk right over to it, not realizing that underneath is a venomous snake. It will see a cliff and wander along its edge, not realizing that a slip of its hoof could send it quickly over the side. They are stubborn in wanting to go their own way.

Likewise, we have gone astray from God. We steal, lust, hate others, use profanity, have unkind thoughts, and are dishonest. We insist on doing what is wrong. But the God who is truthful with us also loves us. An all righteous God must punish sin and that punishment is death. But God punished His Son, Jesus Christ, in our place even though *we* were the ones who sinned. As that verse says, God "laid on *Him* the iniquity of us all." The third day that Son arose from the grave.

God can now pardon us because of what His Son did on our behalf. We have to accept that pardon by placing our trust in Christ as our personal Savior. The moment we do, we are forgiven of all our sin and receive His free gift of eternal life.

The truth hurts – we are sinners deserving of death. But it also helps. If we acknowledge that fact, God can save us from our sin and give us an eternal relationship with Him.

41

Three Questions God is Not Asking You

(using Romans 4:5)

Often when we contemplate having a right relationship with God, we think of God as some kind of interrogation officer. We imagine that He will have some questions for us. While there is indeed one essential question He will ask, I can assure you, the Bible tells us that there are three questions He will *not* ask.

We know for certain what those three questions are based on one sentence in the Bible. In Romans 4:5, God says, "But to him who does not work but believes on Him who justifies the ungodly, his faith is accounted for righteousness."

The first question God is not asking is, "How many good works have you done?" Romans 4:5 begins, "But to him who does not work." If God were to accept us based on what we have done, all He would be doing is giving us something He owes us. An Almighty God will not be in debt to anyone. So, He is not asking, "How many good works have you done?"

A second question He is not asking is, "How well have you behaved?" Romans 4:5 continues, "But believes on Him who justifies the ungodly." It does not matter how well you have behaved; you are still what He calls *un*godly. That means that you are the opposite of everything He is. What's more, it is a matter of believing, not behaving. Jesus Christ, God's perfect Son, paid on a cross for everything ungodly you have done and took the punishment you deserved. The third day He arose from the grave. Since God is godly and you are not, He can only accept the work of His Son—not anything you've done. "Believing" means you trust Jesus Christ alone to save you.

There is a third question God is not asking. That is, "How good a Christian do you promise to be?" The last part of Romans 4:5 says, "his faith is accounted for righteousness." That word "accounted" means to apply something to your account. When you trust Christ, God takes His Son's righteousness and puts it on your account, so when God looks at you, He no longer sees your sin, He sees the perfection of His Son. You stand completely righteous before God and He is not asking, "How good a Christian do you promise to be?"

So, the bottom line is, God has only one question He wants to ask you. Will you trust Christ to save you?

42

Three Things God Cannot Do
(using John 3:16)

We often think, God can do anything. However, there are three things God cannot do. They are found in one sentence of the Bible.

John 3:16 says, "For God so loved the world that He gave His only begotten Son, that whoever believes in Him should not perish but have everlasting life."

First, He cannot love you any more than He has loved you because "God so loved the world." He does not love you with a conditional love that says, "I love you *if,*" but an unconditional love that says, "I love you *period.*" It does not matter who you are, where you have been, or what you have done—He loves you. And He cannot love you any more than He has always loved you.

Second, God cannot give you any more than He has given you, because He gave you His only Son. John 3:16 says, He "gave His only begotten Son." A holy God has to punish sin. God allowed His only Son—the one who was absolutely perfect—to take your punishment and mine on a cross and die in our place. The third day He arose from the grave. God cannot give you any more than He has given you because He gave you His *only* Son.

Third, God cannot make it any simpler than He has made it. John 3:16 says, "that whoever believes in Him should not perish but have everlasting life." That word believe means to trust in Him alone as your only way to heaven. It does not say, whoever goes to church, or whoever lives a good life, or whoever gets baptized. Instead it says, "whoever believes" – anyone who trusts in Him alone as their only way to heaven has everlasting life. When you are able to say Christ died, that's history. When you are able to say, "Christ died for *me,* and I am trusting Him alone to save me," that's salvation. God cannot make it any simpler than that.

There's three things God cannot do. He cannot love you any more than He has loved you because "God so loved the world." He cannot give you any more than He has given you because He gave you His only Son. God cannot make it any simpler than He has made it because whoever believes in Him shall not perish but have everlasting life. Why not let Him save you?

43

Two Kinds of Religion

(using Titus 3:5)

There are two kinds of religion – the kind that you hold, and the kind that holds you.

The kind that you hold is where you come to God and tell Him about when you were baptized, the many good things you have done, the sacraments you have taken, and the commandments you have kept. You bring these to Him as a basis on which He should grant you eternal life.

The problem with that kind of religion is that it does not save. God, through Paul the Apostle, tells us in Titus 3:5, "Not by works of righteousness which we have done, but according to His mercy He saved us." No matter how good you have been or how many good things you have done, those things will never save you.

The good news is there is another kind of religion; it's the religion that *holds you*. This religion is "according to His mercy." We are all sinners and the punishment for sin is eternal separation from God. But the word mercy means God holds back the very thing we deserve. But how could God do that? By allowing His perfect Son Jesus Christ to take the punishment that *we* deserved and die in our place on a cross. He saved us by dying *in our place*. When He arose the third day, that was proof that God accepted His Son's death as total and complete payment for our sins.

That is why we must come to God as sinners, recognize Christ died for us and rose again, and trust in Christ – not in our good life and not even Christ *and* our good life – but trust in Christ alone to save us. The moment we do, God in His mercy gives us eternal life as a free gift. At that moment instead of having a religion we hold, we have a religion that holds us. We are saved not on the basis of what we have done, but on the basis of what He did for us on a cross. He saved us; we were not able to save ourselves.

Two kinds of religion – the one that we hold or the one that holds us. Only the one that holds us saves us, because our trust is in Christ alone as our only basis for eternal life. Which religion do you have?

44

Wealth is Not What You Have But Who You Know
(using 1 Timothy 6:7)

Have you ever thought of the harm a sofa can do? Or a riding lawn mower, car, motorcycle, beach house, tool chest, wardrobe, bank account, set of golf clubs, computer, toys, gadgets, or membership in a country club? Quite an assorted list, right? So, what possible harm could any of those things do? They are merely things.

But *that* is where they can do harm – forgetting that they are *things*. None of which we can take with us when we go.

1 Timothy 6:7 gives a much-needed warning. Simple, but profound. "For we brought nothing into this world, and it is certain we can carry nothing out." We can't take out what we didn't bring in. As someone once noted, "I have never seen a hearse pulling a U-Haul." It's said that without Christ the richest man is poor and with Christ, the poorest man is rich. "Things" can cause us to get distracted from what God considers real wealth.

To God, wealth is not a matter of what you have but who you know. Spiritually, we are bankrupt. Sin comes with a heavy debt, and there is no way we can pay back that debt. Being perfect and just, God will not accept anything short of perfection. So, regardless of any good we have done, we remain sinners who have broken His commandments. That debt, that punishment for those sins, is eternal separation from God.

87

Jesus Christ met us in that condition. As the perfect Son of God, He came to earth and died on a cross, taking the punishment for the debt of all sins of all people. The third day He arose in victory over sin and the grave. Our sin now being paid for, God can give us, as a free-gift, eternal life in the presence of God Himself.

We have to accept that gift by believing – by placing our trust in Christ alone as our only way to heaven. The second we do so, we are immensely rich. All of heaven awaits us. All things will be left behind. We are rich, not on the basis of what we have here, but on the basis of Who we know.

How wealthy are you? Is your wealth in things or in a Person? Wealth is not what you have but Who you know.

45

"Who Am I" Can Be
Answered in Six Words
(using 2 Corinthians 5:17)

We struggle with our identity – that burning question, "Who am I?"

We often point to our ability (whether mental or physical), priding ourselves on our intellect or ability even referencing our educational degrees. Sometimes we point to our achievements, noting our performance for our company as evidenced by promotions and awards. Other times we point to our character, contrasting ourselves with those whose character and conduct leave a lot to be desired.

The problem with all those is their fleeting nature. Abilities or standings within our home, job, or community can change through accident or physical decline. Regardless of our character, we all make mistakes some of which are costly to ourselves or others.

Meaningful and lasting identity can only be found in one place. That is in a person whose name is Jesus Christ. 2 Corinthians 5:17 of the Bible tells us, "Therefore, if anyone is in Christ, he is a new creation; old things have passed away; behold, all things have become new." When we are personally related to Christ, we are a new creation. It doesn't matter what other people think of us, it is how *He thinks* that matters and we are His children forever. All mistakes and failures are a thing of the past. Present failures are always forgiven. We have the ability to live a life we could never live. Instead of evaluating ourselves through other people's eyes, we look at ourselves and all of life through His eyes. To say, "I am the best at what I do" means little or nothing. To say, "I belong to Christ and am a child of God" means everything.

What is exciting is that that identity comes as a free gift. As sinners, we are facing eternal separation from God. Jesus Christ on a cross took the punishment that we should have taken, died in our place and arose the third day. If we come to God acknowledging that we are sinners, but that His Son died for us, and trust His Son to save us from our sin, we are forever His. We can live every day in the excitement of knowing that we are a child of God.

Where do you find your identity? Can you answer that in six words, "I am a child of God"?

46

With God, there is No Longer a Need for "If Only"

(using Philippians 4:11-13)

If only my wife was better at disciplining the children. If only my husband would get his act together. I would be a lot happier, if only my children did not test my patience. Things would go better at work, if only my boss was easier to work for.

Ever notice how much our lives are governed by "If only"?

One of the most exciting things about having a personal relationship with Jesus Christ is that all the "if onlys" can become a thing of the past.

In Philippians 4:11-13, Paul the apostle said, "I have learned in whatever state I am, to be content: I know how to be abased, and I know how to abound. Everywhere and in all things I have learned to be full and to be hungry, both to abound and to suffer need. I can do all things through Christ who strengthens me."

That last sentence actually means, "I can handle all things through Christ who strengthens me." In essence, Paul was saying, "It does not matter if I am at a high or at a low, if I have more than what I think I need or less, if everything is going right or life turns upside down— I can handle it through Christ who strengthens me." The reason is simple. Some circumstances in life are bigger than you are. Nothing and No One is bigger than He is. So, when you have Christ, you can be in control of your circumstances instead of them being in control of you.

But before you can experience Christ, first you have to know Him. Knowing Christ does not mean going to church on a regular basis or living the best life you can. It means coming to God and admitting you are a sinner who deserves eternal separation from God. It means you *know* and recognize that Jesus Christ took the punishment for sin you deserved, died in your place, and arose the third day. Through personal trust in Christ as your only way to heaven, you receive His free gift of eternal life.

Come to Christ now. You will have His presence, through the Holy Spirit, within you. Whatever comes into your life, instead of saying, "If only," you can then say, "Whatever it is, with Christ, I can handle it."

47

You Are Never Too Big a Sinner for God to Save
(using 1 Timothy 1:15,16)

When we think of God and spiritual things, some of us have a deep-seated fear. That is, "I am too big a sinner for God to save." As we think of all the dirty thoughts we have had, the selfish things we have done, moments when our anger was out of control, relationships we have broken, and sexual sins we have committed, we wonder if we are too far gone for God to save.

There are two verses in the Bible that assure you that you are not beyond God's reach. In 1 Timothy 1:15-16, Paul the apostle says, "This is a faithful saying, and worthy of all acceptance, that Christ Jesus came into the world to save sinners, of whom I am chief. However, for this reason I obtained mercy, that in me first Jesus Christ might show all longsuffering, as a pattern for those who are going to believe on Him for everlasting life."

Regardless of what you have done, you would look like a saint compared to Paul prior to his conversion. He hated Christians so much that his philosophy was, "The only good Christian was a dead Christian." He was notorious for persecuting believers and watching their execution.

But God gave him mercy. Paul explains that one reason God did that was so Paul could be a "pattern." That means an example, a sketch, an illustration. Paul was saying that God saved him to prove that if God can save *him*, He can save anyone.

The reason is that on a cross two-thousand years ago, Jesus Christ, the Son of God, did not pay for just some sinners' sins. He paid for everyone's sins. It does not matter whether we have committed just a "little white lie" or the worst sin imaginable. It was paid for by His death on the cross. When He arose the third day, that was proof God accepted His Son's payment for your sins. If you will do what Paul did – believe – that is place your trust in Christ alone to save you, God will give you the free gift of everlasting life.

Paul's testimony was God's way of saying to you, "You are never too big a sinner for God to save." Will you let Him save you?

48

You Can Overcome the Fear of Dying

(using Hebrews 2:14-15)

Sooner or later, it grips us all. It might be when we are getting dressed in the morning and notice an unusual lump underneath our arm. Or it could be when we pass a car accident that looks like it could have been fatal. Or perhaps it is when we receive word that a close friend or relative died unexpectedly at an early age of an undiagnosed heart condition.

I am talking about the fear of death. Something so real that a comedian once said, "I'm not afraid of death. I just don't want to be there when it happens."

The Bible speaks of that fear and the grip it has upon every one of us. Listen to this simple statement from Hebrews 2:14-15. "Inasmuch then as the children have partaken of flesh and blood, He Himself likewise shared in the same, that through death He might destroy him who had the power of death, that is, the devil, and release those who through fear of death were all their lifetime subject to bondage." That sentence is basically saying that the fear of death makes slaves of us all. It often dictates what we do, buy, or how we travel.

God desires to release us from that fear. The sentence reads, "and *release* those who through fear of death were all their lifetime subject to bondage." That word 'release' means to set us free from the fear of death. How did He accomplish that?

Sin is the reason for death. Because we have sinned, we deserve to die physically and be separated from God forever in what the Bible calls hell. God's Son, Jesus Christ, became flesh and blood and took our punishment by dying on a cross in our place. When He arose the third day, that was proof He had conquered sin and the grave. Through simple faith—faith which means trusting Jesus Christ alone as our only way to heaven—we receive complete pardon for our sins and His free gift of eternal life. Eternal life begins the *moment* we trust Christ. So, when death comes, we are immediately transferred into His presence where we will live forever. Death for a Christian is no longer something to be feared but something to look forward to.

Why not come to Christ and shake free of your fear of death?

49

You Cannot Live the Christian Life
(using Galatians 2:20)

There is a fear that keeps some of us from coming to Christ. That fear is about living the Christian life. Our conscience tells us that if we come to Christ we ought to live like a Christian and we fear that we could not do that.

First of all, there is no way you could live the Christian life. But could I encourage you by telling you that God is not expecting you to?

In Galatians 2:20, Paul the apostle spoke to those who have already trusted Christ. He said, "I have been crucified with Christ; it is no longer I who live, but Christ lives in me; and the life which I now live in the flesh I live by faith in the Son of God, who loved me and gave Himself for me."

The Christian life isn't about a life lived for Christ; it is a life in which Christ lives through you.

Notice Paul's words, "the Son of God who loved me and gave Himself for me." On a road to Damascus, Paul was brought to his knees by God Himself and forced to acknowledge that he was a sinner who deserved death and everlasting separation from God. Paul came to see Christ for who He really is – the Son of God who loved him, gave Himself for him, and rose from the grave the third day.

Paul came to understand that if he would simply believe - place his *trust* in Christ alone to save him - God would forgive him of all his sins and give him the free gift of eternal life.

Paul trusted Christ. He became a Christian. But note his words, "the life which I *now live* in the flesh I live by faith in the Son of God." Paul knew that he could not live a different life; God had to live it through him. So, every day he relied upon the Lord to live the life which he could not live. It was not Paul living for Christ, but Christ living through Paul.

God does not expect you to live the Christian life. So, don't let that keep you from coming to Christ. He is asking you to come to Christ and then let Christ live that life through you.

50

Your Final Address

(using 2 Corinthians 5:8)

Every one of us ought to answer the question, "What is going to be your final address?"

I am not referring to the street you live on –those last five seconds before you die because that is not actually your final address. Instead, I am referring to your address –five seconds after you die. The Bible makes it clear that when we die our address will either be heaven or hell. We will either be with God forever or –separated from Him forever.

But do you know what's exciting? You can know *now* that your final address will be heaven. The Apostle Paul had that certainty. So much so, that he could hardly wait to leave his address on earth to go to heaven. He said in 2 Corinthians 5:8, "We are confident, yes, well pleased rather to be absent from the body and to be present with the Lord."

How can you know that your final address will be heaven? Well, unlike the place you are now, your location in heaven cannot be worked for or earned by a life of good behavior, an accumulation of good deeds, or a consistent church attendance-record. Instead, eternal life with Jesus Christ is completely free because of something that happened two thousand years ago.

All of us are sinners. We have broken God's commandments and deserve to be forever separated from God in a place the Bible calls hell. But God so loved us that He sent Jesus Christ into the world to take the punishment for your sins and mine, and to die as our substitute. They crucified Christ where they should have crucified you and me. The third day He arose as proof that God had accepted His sin-payment for our sin-problem.

With our debt of sin paid through Jesus Christ's death in our place, God can now offer a place in heaven for us as a free gift. All *we* have to do is what the Bible calls believe – that means to place your trust in Christ alone as your only way to heaven.

When you come to God as a sinner, recognizing that Jesus Christ died for you and rose again, God gives you eternal life for free. From that point on, know you that the moment you stop living here, you will be with God forever. Your final address will be heaven. Come to Him now.

51

Your Goodness is Not Good Enough
(Using Philippians 3:9)

Ask the average person, "What do you have to do to get to heaven?" Almost everyone would say, "You have to be good."

Now they may differ on what "good" means. Some might define it as loving your neighbor, others as going to church, some as being baptized, others as keeping the commandments, and still others as simply staying out of jail. But there is one thing they all miss that the Bible makes clear. That is that your righteousness—your goodness—is not good enough. You have to be as perfect as Jesus Christ, God's only Son, was. That means regardless of how good you have been, you have not been good enough.

That is why Paul the apostle in the New Testament says in Philippians 3:9, "and be found in Him, not having my own righteousness, which is from the law, but that which is through faith in Christ, the righteousness which is from God by faith." Your goodness will not get you to heaven; you need perfection. And only Christ is perfect.

How do you obtain that perfection? Paul says, you receive it by faith. Faith means "trust." You have to come to God as a sinner who deserves to be separated from God forever. On a cross two-thousand years ago, God's perfect Son died as your substitute, taking that punishment for sin that you deserved. The third day He rose again. Faith means, recognizing that Christ died in your place. You must trust in Christ alone as your only way to heaven,

101

your only means of a right standing with God.

The moment you trust Christ, something miraculous take place. God takes His Son's righteousness, and He clothes you with it. So, when God looks upon you, He no longer sees your sin, He sees the perfection of His Son Christ. You are then forever accepted by God not based on what you have done for Christ, but what He did for you on a cross. You are accepted by God based on His Son's perfection, not based on your goodness. That is why Paul said, "And be found in Him, not having my own righteousness... but that which is through faith in Christ."

Your goodness is not good enough. Never has been. Never will be. Let God accept you based on His Son's perfection by trusting Christ to save you.

52

Your Struggle is from God

(using Ecclesiastes 3:11 and John 17:3)

One of the wealthiest men in America made this comment: "The one thing that bothers me is that I do not know where I am going when I die. I am convinced there's something out there. I just don't know what it is."

Ever have that same struggle? Along with that comes questions about where you find meaning in life. Or, how do you find something that really lasts?

That struggle, that *curiosity*, is God-given. He put it there.

Solomon in the Bible was one of the wisest men who ever lived. In the book of Ecclesiastes, he says, "He has made everything beautiful in its time. Also He has put eternity in their hearts, except that no one can find out the work that God does from beginning to end." God has a divine plan, and—in the grand scheme of things—everything is beautiful, even the events we don't understand at the moment.

But listen to that phrase, "He has put eternity in their hearts." That's referring to that deep inner compulsion we all have, to know what is out there. What is beyond our own mortality? Where do we find meaning in this life, and what's in the hereafter? That struggle is from God. He put it there.

That's why we will only find inner peace when we are in a proper relationship with the Creator. Then we can live with the assurance that we know where we are going when we die and trust Him for whatever happens in our lives. The Scriptures are clear that the only way you can know Him is through His Son Jesus Christ. John 17:3 tells us, "And this is eternal life, that they may know You, the only true God, and Jesus Christ whom You have sent."

God sent His Son Jesus Christ into the world to pay for all the wrongs we have done. He took the punishment for our sins by dying on the cross as our substitute. Then He rose again the third day. When we trust Christ as our personal Savior, we have peace in knowing that we will be with Him forever and in knowing *Him* – the One who is in complete control and understands all there is about life.

Your struggle comes from God. He wants you to discover the One, and only one, who gives meaning to life, now and forever.

ACCIDENTS
You Can Overcome the Fear of Dying   95

ACCUSATIONS
The Mark of a True Friend   67

ADDICTION
Only Jesus Christ Can Break Your Chains   43

ADDRESS
Your Final Address   99

ADULTERY
God Has a Reputation for Making Miracles Out of Messes   25
The Mark of a True Friend   67
Every Marriage Needs a Third Person - of the Right Kind   21

ADULTHOOD
"Come" Tells Us How Many People God Cares For   7

AGING
"Come" Tells Us How Many People God Cares For   7

ALARM
Nothing Is Worth Being Separated from God Over   37

ALCOHOLISM
Only Jesus Christ Can Break Your Chains   43

ANGER
Only Jesus Christ Can Break Your Chains   43

ARROGANCE
The Most Humble Person You Will Ever Meet   69

ASSURANCE
Hope So or Know So Salvation   31
Three Questions God is Not Asking You   81
Two Kinds of Religion   85

ATTITUDE
The Biggest Difference Between Religion and Christ   59
Two Kinds of Religion   85

ATTRACTIONS
The People You are Attracted to the Most | 77

BAD NEWS GOOD NEWS
Bad News, Good News | 3

BAPTISM
Salvation is Not Christ Plus but Christ Period | 45
The Biggest Difference Between Religion and Christ | 59
The Greatest Formula in the Bible | 63
Two Kinds of Religion | 85
Do vs. Done | 13

BARGAINS
Come to Christ and You Will Get Two For the Price of One | 9

BEHAVIOR
Three Questions God is Not Asking You | 81
Two Kinds of Religion | 85
Do vs. Done | 13
God's Love is Not "Iffy" | 29

BETRAYAL
Come to Christ and You Will Get Two For the Price of One | 9

BIBLE
Don't Worry About Parts of the Bible You Don't
Understand; Worry about Those You Do | 19
One Question the Bible Answers Clearly | 41
The Greatest Formula in the Bible | 63

BIRTHDAYS
The Day You Die Ought to be More Exciting
than the Day You Were Born | 61

BLINDNESS
Satan's Primary Goal in Your Life | 47

BLUNDERS
Mislabeling Can Be Dangerous | 35

BONDAGE
Only Jesus Christ Can Break Your Chains | 43
You Can Overcome the Fear of Dying | 95

CELEBRATION
The Day You Die Ought to be More Exciting
than the Day You Were Born   61

CERTAINTY
Hope So or Know So Salvation   31

CHAINS
Only Jesus Christ Can Break Your Chains   43
The Past Can Be a Memory, Not a Nightmare   75

CHARACTER
God Actually is Unfair   23
God's Love is Not "Iffy"   29

CHILD REARING
As A Parent, Tell Your Child About Someone
You Know, Not Someone You Know About   1
With God, There is No Longer a Need for "If Only"   91

CHRISTIAN GROWTH
Come to Christ and You Will Get Two For the Price of One   9

CHRISTIAN LIVING
Come to Christ and You Will Get Two For the Price of One   9
You Cannot Live the Christian Life   97

CHRISTIANITY
The Biggest Difference Between Religion and Christ   59
Christianity is about a Message, Not a Messenger   5

CHRISTIANS
Christianity is about a Message, Not a Messenger   5

CHRISTMAS
The Most Important Word in the Christmas Story   71

CHURCH
Salvation is Not Christ Plus but Christ Period   45
The Biggest Difference Between Religion and Christ   59
The Greatest Formula in the Bible   63
Two Kinds of Religion   85
Your Goodness is Not Good Enough   101

CHURCH
Christianity is about a Message, Not a Messenger 5
Do vs. Done 13

CIRCUMSTANCES
With God, There is No Longer a Need for "If Only" 91

CLARITY
One Question the Bible Answers Clearly 41
The Biggest Difference Between Religion and Christ 59
The Greatest Formula in the Bible 63
Three Things God Cannot Do 83
"Who Am I" Should Be Answered in Six Words 89

CLASSIFICATIONS
God Has a Reputation for Making Miracles Out of Messes 25

COMFORT
Satisfaction is Found in a Person, not Possessions 49

COMMANDMENTS
Salvation is Not Christ Plus but Christ Period 45
The Biggest Difference Between Religion and Christ 59
Two Kinds of Religion 85
Do vs. Done 13

COMMUNION
The Lord's Table Looks Three Ways 65

CONCEIT
The Most Humble Person You Will Ever Meet 69

CONFUSION
Don't Worry About Parts of the Bible You
Don't Understand; Worry about Those You Do 19
God Actually is Unfair 23
One Question the Bible Answers Clearly 41
Talk to the Person Who Lives There 51
The Biggest Difference Between Religion and Christ 59
The Greatest Formula in the Bible 63
Three Things God Cannot Do 83

CONSCIENCE
The Past Can Be a Memory, Not a Nightmare 75

CONTENTMENT
Satisfaction is Found in a Person, not Possessions 49

CURIOSITY
Your Struggle is From God 103

DAMAGE
Satan's Primary Goal in Your Life 47

DEATH
One Question the Bible Answers Clearly 41
The Best is Yet to Come 55
The Best Way I Can Use My Tongue 57
The Day You Die Ought to be More Exciting
than the Day You Were Born 61
You Can Overcome the Fear of Dying 95
Your Final Address 99
Your Struggle is From God 103
God's Love is Not "Iffy" 29
Wealth is Not What You Have, But Who You Know 87

DEBT
Do vs. Done 13

DECEIT
Do Yourself a Favor 15

DECEPTION
Satan's Primary Goal in Your Life 47

DECISIONS
Don't Put Off Till Tomorrow What You Should Do Today 17
It's Your Move 33
Your Final Address 99

DEFEAT
You Can Overcome the Fear of Dying 95
You Cannot Live the Christian Life 97

DEFINITION
The Best Definition and Example of Love   53

DELAY
Don't Put Off Till Tomorrow What You Should Do Today   17
Nothing Is Worth Being Separated from God Over   37

DESIRE
God's Greatest Desire for Your Life   27

DESPAIR
You Are Never Too Big a Sinner for God to Save   93
You Cannot Live the Christian Life   97

DEVIL
You Can Overcome the Fear of Dying   95

DIRECTIONS
Talk to the Person Who Lives There   51

DISAPPOINTMENTS
Come to God and You Will Meet the   11
Promise-Keeper, Not the Promise Breaker

DISTRACTIONS
Nothing Is Worth Being Separated from God Over   37
Wealth is Not What You Have, But Who You Know   87

DOUBT
Do Yourself a Favor   15
Hope So or Know So Salvation   31
One Question the Bible Answers Clearly   41

DOWN PAYMENT
Do vs. Done   13

DRUGS
Only Jesus Christ Can Break Your Chains   43

DRUNKENNESS
God Has a Reputation for Making Miracles Out of Messes   25

ELDERLY
"Come" Tells Us How Many People God Cares For 7

EMBARRASSMENT
God's Love is Not "Iffy" 29

ERROR
Mislabeling Can Be Dangerous 35

ETERNITY
It's Your Move 33
One Question the Bible Answers Clearly 41
The Day You Die Ought to be More Exciting
than the Day You Were Born 61
You Can Overcome the Fear of Dying 95
Your Final Address 99
Your Struggle is From God 103

EXAMINATION
Do Yourself a Favor 15
Don't Worry About Parts of the Bible You
Don't Understand; Worry about Those You Do 19

EXAMPLE
The Best Definition and Example of Love 53

EXCITEMENT
The Day You Die Ought to be More Exciting
than the Day You Were Born 61

EXPECTATIONS
God's Greatest Desire for Your Life 27
God's Love is Not "Iffy" 29

FAILURE
God Has a Reputation for Making Miracles Out of Messes 25
You Cannot Live the Christian Life 97
Your Goodness is Not Good Enough 101

FAIRNESS
God Actually is Unfair 23

FAME
Satisfaction is Found in a Person, not Possessions   49

FAMILY
Every Marriage Needs a Third Person - of the Right Kind   21
With God, There is No Longer a Need for "If Only"   91

FATALITIES
You Can Overcome the Fear of Dying   95

FAVORS
Do Yourself a Favor   15

FEAR
You Are Never Too Big a Sinner for God to Save   93
You Can Overcome the Fear of Dying   95
You Cannot Live the Christian Life   97

FINANCES
Wealth is Not What You Have, But Who You Know   87

FLAWS
Mislabeling Can Be Dangerous   35

FORGIVENESS
The Best is Yet to Come   55
The Past Can Be a Memory, Not a Nightmare   75
The Truth Hurts, But It Also Helps   79

FORMULAS
The Greatest Formula in the Bible   63

FORNICATION
God Has a Reputation for Making Miracles Out of Messes   25

FREEDOM
Only Jesus Christ Can Break Your Chains   43

FRIENDSHIP
The Mark of a True Friend   67
The Most Important Word in the Christmas Story   71
The People You are Attracted to the Most   77

FRUSTRATION
One Question the Bible Answers Clearly   41

FUTURE
Don't Put Off Till Tomorrow What You Should Do Today   17
The Best is Yet to Come   55
The Lord's Table Looks Three Ways   65
The Past Can Be a Memory, Not a Nightmare   75

GIFTS
One Gift You Can Never Lose   39
The Best Way I Can Use My Tongue   57
Three Things God Cannot Do   83

GOAL
Satan's Primary Goal in Your Life   47

GODLINESS
Come to Christ and You Will Get Two
For the Price of One   9

GOOD WORKS
Don't Worry About Parts of the Bible
You Don't Understand; Worry about Those You Do   19
Hope So or Know So Salvation   31
Salvation is Not Christ Plus but Christ Period   45
The Biggest Difference Between Religion and Christ   59
The Greatest Formula in the Bible   63
Three Questions God is Not Asking You   81
Two Kinds of Religion   85
Your Goodness is Not Good Enough   101
Do vs. Done   13
Satisfaction is Found in a Person, not Possessions   49
Nothing Is Worth Being Separated from God Over   37
With God, There is No Longer a Need for "If Only"   91

GRACE
Come to Christ and You Will Get Two For the Price of One   9
Don't Worry About Parts of the Bible You Don't
Understand; Worry about Those You Do   19
Mislabeling Can Be Dangerous   35
Three Things God Cannot Do

GUARANTEES
Hope So or Know So Salvation   31
One Question the Bible Answers Clearly   41

HAPPINESS
Satisfaction is Found in a Person, not Possessions   49

HARDSHIP
God Actually is Unfair   23

HEALTH
Satisfaction is Found in a Person, not Possessions   49
Wealth is Not What You Have, But Who You Know   87

HEAVEN
Hope So or Know So Salvation   31
Salvation is Not Christ Plus but Christ Period   45
Satan's Primary Goal in Your Life   47
Talk to the Person Who Lives There   51
The Best is Yet to Come   55
The Day You Die Ought to be More Exciting
than the Day You Were Born   61
Your Final Address   99
Your Goodness is Not Good Enough   101

HELL
Your Final Address   99
Nothing Is Worth Being Separated from God Over   37

HEREAFTER
One Question the Bible Answers Clearly   41
The Best is Yet to Come   55
Your Struggle is From God   103

HOLINESS
The One Thing That Stands Between You and God   73

HOME
Talk to the Person Who Lives There   51

HOMOSEXUALITY
God Has a Reputation for Making Miracles Out of Messes   25

HONESTY
The Truth Hurts, But It Also Helps   79

HOPELESSNESS
Only Jesus Christ Can Break Your Chains   43
You Are Never Too Big a Sinner for God to Save   93
You Cannot Live the Christian Life   97

HUMILITY
The Most Humble Person You Will Ever Meet   69

HUSBAND
Every Marriage Needs a Third Person - of the Right Kind   21

HYPOCRISY
The One Thing That Stands Between You and God   73
Christianity is about a Message, Not a Messenger   5

IDENTITY
"Who Am I" Should Be Answered in Six Words   89

IDOLATRY
God Has a Reputation for Making Miracles Out of Messes   25

IMPOSTERS
Do Yourself a Favor   15

INFLUENCE
The Day You Die Ought to be More Exciting
than the Day You Were Born   61
Satisfaction is Found in a Person, not Possessions   49

INSUFFICIENCY
Salvation is Not Christ Plus but Christ Period   45

INTEGRITY
The Mark of a True Friend   67
The Truth Hurts, But It Also Helps   79

INTERROGATION
Three Questions God is Not Asking You   81

INVITATIONS
"Come" Tells Us How Many People God Cares For   7

JUSTIFICATION
God Has a Reputation for Making Miracles Out of Messes   25
Three Questions God is Not Asking You   81

LANGUAGE
The Best Way I Can Use My Tongue   57

LEADER
The Most Important Word in the Christmas Story   71

LEGACY
The Day You Die Ought to be More Exciting than
the Day You Were Born   61

LIES
Satan's Primary Goal in Your Life   47
The Truth Hurts, But It Also Helps   79
With God, There is No Longer a Need for "If Only"   91

LIFE
God's Greatest Desire for Your Life   27
Satan's Primary Goal in Your Life   47
The Best Way I Can Use My Tongue   57
The Day You Die Ought to be More Exciting
than the Day You Were Born   61
Nothing Is Worth Being Separated from God Over   37

LIFESTYLE
God's Love is Not "Iffy"   29

LISTENING
The One Thing That Stands Between You and God   73

LORD'S SUPPER
The Lord's Table Looks Three Ways   65

LOSS
One Gift You Can Never Lose   39
God's Love is Not "Iffy"   29

LOVE
The Best Definition and Example of Love   53
The People You are Attracted to the Most   77
Three Things God Cannot Do   83

LOVE
God's Love is Not "Iffy"   29

LYING
Come to God and You Will Meet the
Promise-Keeper, Not the Promise Breaker   11

MAIL
Don't Worry About Parts of the Bible You
Don't Understand; Worry about Those You Do   19

MARRIAGE
Every Marriage Needs a Third Person - The Right Kind   21
With God, There is No Longer a Need for "If Only"   91

MATERIALISM
The Best is Yet to Come   55
Your Struggle is From God   103
Satisfaction is Found in a Person, not Possessions   49
Nothing Is Worth Being Separated from God Over   37
Wealth is Not What You Have, But Who You Know   87

MEMORIALS
The Lord's Table Looks Three Ways   65

MEMORY
The Past Can Be a Memory, Not a Nightmare   75

MERCY
The Biggest Difference Between Religion and Christ   59
Two Kinds of Religion   85

MESSAGE
Christianity is about a Message, Not a Messenger   5

MESSENGER
Christianity is about a Message, Not a Messenger   5

MESSES
God Has a Reputation for Making Miracles Out of Messes   25

MIND
The Past Can Be a Memory, Not a Nightmare   75

MIRACLES
God Actually is Unfair   23
God Has a Reputation for Making Miracles Out of Messes   25

MISLABELING
Mislabeling Can Be Dangerous   35

MISTAKE
Mislabeling Can Be Dangerous   35

MISUNDERSTANDING
Three Questions God is Not Asking You   81
Three Things God Cannot Do   83

MONEY
Your Struggle is From God   103
Satisfaction is Found in a Person, not Possessions   49
Wealth is Not What You Have, But Who You Know   87

MORTALITY
Your Struggle is From God   103

NIGHTMARE
The Past Can Be a Memory, Not a Nightmare   75

OLD AGE
"Come" Tells Us How Many People God Cares For   7

OPTIMISM
You Are Never Too Big a Sinner for God to Save   93

PAIN
The Best is Yet to Come   55

PARENTING
As A Parent, Tell Your Child About Someone
You Know, Not Someone You Know About   1

PARENTING
With God, There is No Longer a Need for "If Only"   91

PASSIONS
Come to Christ and You Will Get Two For the Price of One   9

PAST
The Best is Yet to Come   55
You Are Never Too Big a Sinner for God to Save   93
The Lord's Table Looks Three Ways   65
The Past Can Be a Memory, Not a Nightmare   75
With God, There is No Longer a Need for "If Only"   91

PEACE
Satisfaction is Found in a Person, not Possessions   49

PERFECTION
Your Goodness is Not Good Enough   101

PERFORMANCE
Salvation is Not Christ Plus but Christ Period   45
Three Questions God is Not Asking You   81
Do vs. Done   13
God's Love is Not "Iffy"   29

PERSONALITY
God's Love is Not "Iffy"   29

PERSPECTIVE
The Lord's Table Looks Three Ways   65

PESSIMISM
You Are Never Too Big a Sinner for God to Save   93

PLANNING
Don't Put Off Till Tomorrow What You Should Do Today   17
It's Your Move   33
Nothing Is Worth Being Separated from God Over   37

PLEASURE
Satisfaction is Found in a Person, not Possessions   49

POPULARITY
"Who Am I" Should Be Answered in Six Words   89

PORNOGRAPHY
Only Jesus Christ Can Break Your Chains   43

POSSESSIONS
Your Struggle is From God   103
Satisfaction is Found in a Person, not Possessions   49
Wealth is Not What You Have, But Who You Know   87

POWER
Only Jesus Christ Can Break Your Chains   43
The Best Way I Can Use My Tongue   57
Satisfaction is Found in a Person, not Possessions   49

PRESENT
Don't Put Off Till Tomorrow What You Should Do Today   17
Nothing Is Worth Being Separated from God Over   37

PRIDE
The Most Humble Person You Will Ever Meet   69

PRIORITIES
Nothing Is Worth Being Separated from God Over   37

PROCRASTINATION
Don't Put Off Till Tomorrow What You Should Do Today   17
Nothing Is Worth Being Separated from God Over   37

PROMISES
Three Questions God is Not Asking You   81
Come to God and You Will Meet the
Promise-Keeper, Not the Promise Breaker   11
God's Love is Not "Iffy"   29

PROOF
Do Yourself a Favor   15

PROPITIATION
The Best Definition and Example of Love   53

PROSPERITY
The Best is Yet to Come   55

PURPOSE
God's Greatest Desire for Your Life   27
Your Struggle is From God   103

QUESTIONS
One Question the Bible Answers Clearly   41
Three Questions God is Not Asking You   81
Your Final Address   99

REGRETS
You Are Never Too Big a Sinner for God to Save   93
The Past Can Be a Memory, Not a Nightmare   75
With God, There is No Longer a Need for "If Only"   91

RELATIONSHIPS
The Mark of a True Friend   67
The People You are Attracted to the Most   77
You Are Never Too Big a Sinner for God to Save   93
Every Marriage Needs a Third Person - of the Right Kind   21

RELIGION
The Biggest Difference Between Religion and Christ   59
Two Kinds of Religion   85
Christianity is about a Message, Not a Messenger   5

REMEDIES
Only Jesus Christ Can Break Your Chains   43

REPUTATION
God Has a Reputation for Making Miracles Out of Messes   25
God's Love is Not "Iffy"   29
"Who Am I" Should Be Answered in Six Words   89

REQUIREMENT
The Best Definition and Example of Love   53

RESUMES
God Has a Reputation for Making Miracles Out of Messes   25

RUINATION
God Has a Reputation for Making Miracles Out of Messes 25

SACRAMENTS
Salvation is Not Christ Plus but Christ Period 45
The Biggest Difference Between Religion and Christ 59
The Greatest Formula in the Bible 63
The One Thing That Stands Between You and God 73

SACRAMENTS
Two Kinds of Religion 85
Do vs. Done 13

SACRIFICE
The Best Definition and Example of Love 53
The Lord's Table Looks Three Ways 65

SALINIFICATION
The Best is Yet to Come 55

SANCTIFICATION
God Has a Reputation for Making Miracles Out of Messes 25
The Best Definition and Example of Love 53

SATAN
Satan's Primary Goal in Your Life 47

SATISFACTION
Satisfaction is Found in a Person, not Possessions 49
"Who Am I" Should Be Answered in Six Words 89
With God, There is No Longer a Need for "If Only" 91

SCHEDULING
Don't Put Off Till Tomorrow What You Should Do Today 17
Nothing Is Worth Being Separated from God Over 37

SECURITY
One Gift You Can Never Lose 39

SELF IMAGE
"Who Am I" Should Be Answered in Six Words 89

SELF WORTH
"Who Am I" Should Be Answered in Six Words   89

SELF-ESTEEM
"Who Am I" Should Be Answered in Six Words   89

SELFISHNESS
The Best Definition and Example of Love   53
The Most Humble Person You Will Ever Meet   69
The People You are Attracted to the Most   77

SELFISHNESS
"Who Am I" Should Be Answered in Six Words   89

SEPARATION
The One Thing That Stands Between You and God   73
Nothing Is Worth Being Separated from God Over   37

SHAME
God's Love is Not "Iffy"   29

SIMPLICITY
The Greatest Formula in the Bible   63
Three Things God Cannot Do   83
"Who Am I" Should Be Answered in Six Words   89

SIN
Mislabeling Can Be Dangerous   35
The One Thing That Stands Between You and God   73
The Truth Hurts, But It Also Helps   79

SLAVERY
Only Jesus Christ Can Break Your Chains   43

SORROW
The Best is Yet to Come   55

SPEECH
The Best Way I Can Use My Tongue   57

SPIRITUALITY
The Biggest Difference Between Religion and Christ   59

STRENGTHS
God's Love is Not "Iffy"   29

STRUGGLES
Your Struggle is From God   103

STUDY
Do Yourself a Favor   15
Don't Worry About Parts of the Bible You
Don't Understand; Worry about Those You Do   19

SUFFERING
God Actually is Unfair   23
One Question the Bible Answers Clearly   41

SUFFICIENCY
Salvation is Not Christ Plus but Christ Period   45
Your Goodness is Not Good Enough   101
With God, There is No Longer a Need for "If Only"   91

SURPRISES
Three Questions God is Not Asking You   81

SURRENDER
The Most Humble Person You Will Ever Meet   69

SURVEY
Hope So or Know So Salvation   31

TEACHER
The Most Important Word in the Christmas Story   71

TEMPTATIONS
Only Jesus Christ Can Break Your Chains   43

THEFT
God Has a Reputation for Making Miracles Out of Messes   25

TOMORROW
Don't Put Off Till Tomorrow What You Should Do Today   17

TONGUE
The Best Way I Can Use My Tongue   57

TORMENT
Your Struggle is From God   103

TRUST
Talk to the Person Who Lives There   51

TRUTH
Do Yourself a Favor   15
The Truth Hurts, But It Also Helps   79

TRUTHFULNESS
Come to God and You Will Meet the
Promise-Keeper, Not the Promise Breaker   11
The Truth Hurts, But It Also Helps   79

UNFAIRNESS
God Actually is Unfair   23

UNGODLINESS
Come to Christ and You Will Get Two For the Price of One   9
Three Questions God is Not Asking You   81

VICTIM
Only Jesus Christ Can Break Your Chains   43

VICTORY
Only Jesus Christ Can Break Your Chains   43
You Can Overcome the Fear of Dying   95
You Cannot Live the Christian Life   97

WAITING
Don't Put Off Till Tomorrow What You Should Do Today   17

WEAKNESS
Mislabeling Can Be Dangerous   35
Only Jesus Christ Can Break Your Chains   43
God's Love is Not "Iffy"   29

WEALTH
Your Struggle is From God   103
Satisfaction is Found in a Person, not Possessions   49
Wealth is Not What You Have, But Who You Know   87

WEDDING
Every Marriage Needs a Third Person - of the Right Kind   21

WICKEDNESS
God Has a Reputation for Making Miracles Out of Messes   25

WIFE
Every Marriage Needs a Third Person - of the Right Kind   21

WILL OF GOD
God's Greatest Desire for Your Life   27

WORDS
The Best Way I Can Use My Tongue   57

WORRY
Don't Worry About Parts of the Bible You
Don't Understand; Worry about Those You Do   19

WORSHIP
The Lord's Table Looks Three Ways   65

YOUTH
"Come" Tells Us How Many People God Cares For   7

GENESIS 2:24
Every Marriage Needs a Third Person - of the Right Kind   21

GENESIS 6:5-8
Mislabeling Can Be Dangerous   35

JOB 14:14
One Question the Bible Answers Clearly   41

PSALMS 16:10
Christianity is about a Message, Not a Messenger   5

PROVERBS 18:21A
The Best Way I Can Use My Tongue   57

ECCLESIASTES 2:10-11
Satisfaction is Found in a Person, not Possessions   49

ECCLESIASTES 3:11
Your Struggle is From God   103

ECCLESIASTES 7:1
The Day You Die Ought to be More Exciting
than the Day You Were Born   61

ISAIAH 53:5
Christianity is about a Message, Not a Messenger   5

ISAIAH 53:6
The Truth Hurts, But It Also Helps   79

ISAIAH 59:1-2
The One Thing That Stands Between You and God   73

ISAIAH 7:14
Come to God and You Will Meet the
Promise-Keeper, Not the Promise-Breaker   11

MATTHEW 1:22-23
Come to God and You Will Meet the
Promise-Keeper, Not the Promise-Breaker   11

SCRIPTURE INDEX

MATTHEW 11:28
"Come" Tells Us How Many People God Cares For 7

MARK 9:43-48
Nothing is Worth Being Separated from God Over 37

LUKE 18:9-14
The Biggest Difference Between Religion and Christ 59

LUKE 19:5-6
The People You are Attracted to the Most 77

LUKE 2:11
The Most Important Word in the Christmas Story 71

JOHN 1:11-12
It's Your Move 33

JOHN 3:16
The People You are Attracted to the Most 77
Three Things God Cannot Do 83

JOHN 5:24
The Greatest Formula in the Bible 63

JOHN 5:39
God's Greatest Desire for Your Life 27

JOHN 6:35
Satisfaction is Found in a Person, not Possessions 49

JOHN 6:40
God's Greatest Desire for Your Life 27

JOHN 6:47
Come to God and You Will Meet the
Promise-Keeper, Not the Promise-Breaker 11
Salvation is Not Christ Plus, but Christ Period 45

JOHN 8:36
Only Jesus Christ Can Break Your Chains 43

JOHN 8:7
The Mark of a True Friend 67

JOHN 10:28
One Gift You Can Never Lose 39

JOHN 11:25-26
One Question the Bible Answers Clearly 41

JOHN 14:19
One Question the Bible Answers Clearly 41

JOHN 14:2-3,6
Talk to the Person Who Lives There 51

JOHN 17:3
Your Struggle is From God 103

JOHN 19:30
Do vs Done 13

ACTS 10:43
The Past Can Be a Memory Not a Nightmare 75

ROMANS 1:4
Do Yourself a Favor 15

ROMANS 3:23
Bad News, Good News 3

ROMANS 4:5
Three Questions God is Not Asking You 81

ROMANS 5:8
Bad News, Good News 3

ROMANS 6:23
Bad News Good News 3

ROMANS 8:38-39
God's Love is Not "Iffy" 29

1 CORINTHIANS 11:23-29
The Lord's Table Looks Three Ways   65

1 CORINTHIANS 15:3-5
Christianity is about a Message, Not a Messenger   5

1 CORINTHIANS 6:9-11
God Has a Reputation for Making Miracles out of Messes   25

2 CORINTHIANS 4:3-4
Satan's Primary Goal in Your Life   47

2 CORINTHIANS 5:15
"Come" Tells Us How Many People God Cares For   7

2 CORINTHIANS 5:17
"Who Am I" Can Be Answered in Six Words   89

2 CORINTHIANS 5:21
God Actually is Unfair   23

2 CORINTHIANS 5:8
Your Final Address   99

GALATIANS 2:20
You Cannot Live the Christian Life   97

EPHESIANS 2:8-9
Bad News, Good News   3
Don't Worry About Parts of the Bible You
Don't Understand; Worry about Those You Do   19

EPHESIANS 5:33
Every Marriage Needs a Third Person - of the Right Kind   21

EPHESIANS 6:4
As a Parent, Tell Your Child About Someone
You Know, Not Someone You Know About   1

PHILIPPIANS 2:8
The Most Humble Person You Will Ever Meet   69

PHILIPPIANS 3:9
Your Goodness is Not Good Enough   101

PHILIPPIANS 4:11-13
With God There is No Longer a Need for "If Only"   91

1 TIMOTHY 1:15,16
You Are Never Too Big a Sinner for God to Save   93

1 TIMOTHY 6:7
Wealth to God is Not What You Have But Who You Know   87

TITUS 2:11-13
Come to Christ and You Will Get Two For the Price of One   9

TITUS 3:5
Two Kinds of Religion   85

HEBREWS 2:14-15
You Can Overcome the Fear of Dying   95

JAMES 4:13-14
Don't Put Off Till Tomorrow What You Should Do Today   17

1 JOHN 4:10
The Best Definition and Example of Love   53

1 JOHN 5:13
Hope So or Know So Salvation   31

REVELATION 21:4-5
The Best is Yet to Come   55

GET EQUIPPED & ENCOURAGED

AT EVANTELL.ORG

TAKE OUR FREE PERSONAL EVANGELISM ONLINE COURSES

SEE ALL COURSES AT
EVANTELL.ORG/ONLINE-TRAINING

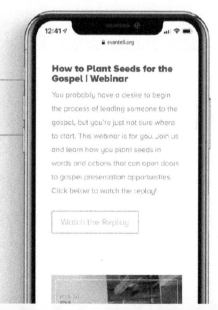

VIEW OUR TOPIC-BASED TRAINING LIBRARY

BROWSE HOURS OF
CONTENT THAT COVER THE
HOTTEST TOPICS AT
EVANTELL.ORG/VIRTUAL-EVENTS

DOWNLOAD OUR APP
FOR EVANGELISM TRAINING
ON-THE-GO

VISIT YOUR APP STORE
AND SEARCH *"EVANTELL"* TO
DOWNLOAD TODAY

VISIT OUR STORE
FOR BOOKS, TRACTS,
AND MORE RESOURCES

VISIT *EVANTELL.ORG/STORE* TO SEE OUR FULL
COLLECTION OF BOOKS AND RESOURCES

Lightning Source UK Ltd.
Milton Keynes UK
UKHW020937150822
407319UK00011B/2072

9 781733 050562